Ralph Nader

Ralph Nader speaks at the U.S. Capitol Building in Washington, D.C.

Ralph Nader

Battling for Democracy

Kevin Graham

Windom Publishing Company

Published by Windom Publishing Company

Windom Publishing Company
PO Box 102225
Denver, CO 80250
(303) 758-3868
www.naderbiography.com
e-mail: windompublishing@yahoo.com

Graham, Kevin, 1959–
    Ralph Nader: battling for democracy/Kevin
Graham — 1st ed.
    p. cm.
    Includes bibliographical references and index.
    ISBN: 0-9700323-0-7

    1. Nader, Ralph—Juvenile literature.
    2. Consumer protection—United States—Biography—
Juvenile literature. 3. Environmentalists—United
States—Biography—Juvenile literature.
    I. Title

    HC110.C63G73 2000   381.34'092
                    QBI00-420

This book is available at special discounts when purchased in bulk quantities for schools, associations, institutions, businesses, organizations or promotions. For more information, please call Windom Publishing Co. at (303) 758-3868 or (800) 850-7094 or visit www.naderbiography.com.

International Standard Book Number (ISBN): 0-9700323-0-7
Library of Congress Control Number: 00-132990

Cover and Interior Design by Lex Papesh
Cover Photo by David Graham

Printed in the United States of America
6 5 4 3 2

For Kathy, Aaron and Lex

Table of

Contents

Chapter One

Surveillance

A sense of unease swept over Ralph Nader.

Eyes watched him from behind. Again. The same eyes belonging to the same man who'd lurked nearby since Nader's arrival in Iowa a few days earlier.

"Is this guy after me?" Nader wondered as he glanced back down the hall and slipped into his hotel room, a current of fear flowing through him.

The answer, he learned soon enough, was yes.

Nader traveled to Des Moines, the state capital, in January 1966 to attend some of the first automobile safety hearings ever held in the United States. Iowa's attorney general, Lawrence Scalise, had called the hearings and personally invited Nader to attend.

A crowd of media people and other witnesses gathered for the proceedings in a cavernous auditorium at the Kirkwood Hotel. Nader testified about various safety problems with automobiles. American car manufacturers took the brunt of his criticisms, as well as those leveled by other witnesses.

"These hearings really shook Detroit up," Nader says, referring to the country's large automakers, all based in Detroit, Mich. "They were really outraged."

But outraged enough to spy on and investigate a lone individual who merely spoke out against their products?

These were turbulent times in the United States. The Vietnam War raged, as did demonstrations against U.S. involvement in the conflict. Civil rights marches in the South stirred further unrest in the country. With all this trouble boiling up in the American public, Nader couldn't be absolutely sure why he was being followed. But he was concerned.

J ust a few months earlier, Nader had finished writing a book about the automobile industry titled *Unsafe at Any Speed.* It severely criticized the industry for building unsafe cars and failing to protect the public. People were dying because car companies were not incorporating safety features. The book garnered lots of attention in newspapers and other media after its publication in November 1965.

The New York Times placed a story about the book on its front page, and a popular Canadian television show broadcast a piece about the book's unsettling conclusions. Just a month before the Iowa hearings, *The Wall Street Journal* favorably reviewed the book. *Unsafe at Any Speed* rose to fifth on the national bestseller list and eventually sold more than half a million copies.

Before and after the Iowa hearings, Nader worked as an unpaid volunteer adviser to a congressional committee in Washington, D.C. The committee was considering new traffic and automobile safety laws. Abraham Ribicoff, a U.S. senator from Connecticut, headed the committee, which also included Senator Robert F. Kennedy and other senators.

After the Iowa gathering, Ribicoff announced a new set of autosafety hearings for his committee, at which Nader would be a main witness. The Ribicoff committee's work drew increased attention from the media with the publication of Nader's book and the Iowa hearings. That attention reflected poorly on American automakers.

Meanwhile, as Nader continued his nonstop work to force the auto industry to manufacture safer cars, he continued to be harassed, spied upon and even intimidated by unknown sources. What was going on?

The phone kept ringing in the middle of the night at Nader's apartment in Washington, D.C. – actually just a single room he rented at a boardinghouse. One caller threatened Nader, saying, "Why don't you go back to Connecticut, buddy boy?" before hanging up. "You're fighting a losing battle, friend," another caller said. "You can't win. You can only lose."

Other calls made no sense at all. Callers claimed they were from an airline or shipping company and asked about mysterious packages before simply hanging up.

In addition, unknown women approached Nader on several occasions. One evening, while Nader strolled the cookie aisle of a grocery store, an attractive woman walked up to him. In a very friendly manner, she asked if he would come up to her apartment to help her move something heavy. When Nader declined, he noticed she didn't bother to ask anyone else in the store for help. She just left.

A similar encounter followed a few days later in a drugstore. Nader again declined the woman's invitation, but he wondered about these chance meetings. He eventually decided they were intended to trap him in an awkward situation.

Nader finally had the chance to prove to himself that, indeed, he was being tailed. At the airport in Philadelphia, after eyeing two men eyeing him, he waited until the last possible moment before boarding his flight. Of course, as soon as he headed into the plane, the two men followed him aboard.

Ralph Nader as a young man in the 1960s.

"I didn't know who they were," Nader says. "It was a mystery – a real concern – and the anonymous phone calls were a little unnerving. I even started using payphones because I figured my phones were bugged."

S oon, however, the investigation of Ralph Nader became public knowledge and a national news story. Detectives conducting the surveillance blundered. They revealed that they were tailing Nader.

Here's how they made their big mistake:

Nader attended the Ribicoff committee hearings in the Senate Office Building. He returned to the building the next day for a television interview. He walked into an elevator and pushed a button to go down. The detectives following him, however, entered a different elevator and went up. When they couldn't find Nader, they approached a security guard in the building, perhaps thinking a police officer would be happy to help them.

"We're detectives. Can you tell us which way Ralph Nader went?" they asked the guard.

"What are you doing? We don't allow this here," responded the guard, who knew of Nader and also knew of a federal law making it a crime to intimidate federal witnesses. The guard, in fact, was studying to become a lawyer. He took down the detectives' names.

The detectives' mistake then grew larger. The security guard, spotting the man he thought was Nader, told him about the detectives. That man, however, was actually a writer for *The Washington Post*. His newspaper published a short article about the mix-up the next day.

That story spurred a reporter in Detroit to ask all the large automakers if they were conducting an investigation of their critic,

Ralph Nader. All of the companies flatly denied the claim except General Motors, which issued a vague response of "no comment."

The case of the mysterious investigation was about to be solved.

"The surveillance became so amateurish in the end that it was almost like slapstick comedy," Nader says, remembering the hubbub caused by the now-revealed investigation. "During that time, it was a race to see who could get which witnesses to testify about the issue of auto safety, and who could get which newspapers to report favorably on the matter. It was a hunt, and I was going after them [the automakers]. Although I was worried about the surveillance, I didn't let it chase me away. If anything, it made me more insistent."

What followed has become a famous bit of recent American history. It's a story of a David taking on a Goliath. And as in the Bible, David – or Ralph Nader, in this case – won.

The eventual revelation that General Motors, one of the world's largest corporations, had investigated the life and habits of an individual critic made big news across the country. The investigation's scope alarmed both Ribicoff's committee and the general public.

Detectives watched Nader's every move over a period of several months – in details such as "subject goes into bank, subject cashes a $50 check, subject leaves and walks down sidewalk." They also interviewed many of Nader's friends and acquaintances. And the questions they asked these people weren't always just about his professional work.

General Motors' aim, according to Nader, had been to get him out of the way – to make him go away. Discovering something bad about Nader's character or lifestyle could make that possible. In fact, one of the detectives conducting the investigation had secretly recorded the company's instructions to him.

A transcript of the conversation, which he later presented in court proceedings, quoted a source as saying, "They [General

Motors] want to get something, somewhere, on this guy to get him out of their hair…There's something somewhere…Find it so they can shut him up."

The detectives looked and searched and dug. They asked Nader's friends all kinds of personal questions. What were his drinking habits? What hours did he keep? Why wasn't he married? Did he take drugs? Was he a homosexual? Was he anti-Semitic? And on and on.

"This confirmed to me their guilt – that they were trying to smear me rather than answer me," Nader says. "I thought, 'Boy, these guys really have a lot to hide.' They were that desperate."

In the end, the investigation revealed nothing dark or unseemly about Nader's character or the way he lived. In fact, it simply showed him to be an aggressive young lawyer with a burning desire to serve the public's needs.

It did, however, reveal something about the operations of one of America's largest and best-known corporations. Ribicoff and his congressional committee members wanted some answers. They called for another hearing in March 1966. They sought an explanation of the alleged harassment of a Senate committee witness: Ralph Nader.

The Hearing

The packed Senate Caucus Room buzzed with anticipation. A bank of television cameras, topped with bright lights, focused on the senators. A horde of media people huddled with their piles of recording equipment. Wires and cables for the equipment ran spaghetti-like around the room. The reporters were crammed into the room with numerous other interested parties and members of the public – all curious to see if high drama would unfold.

Chairman Ribicoff opened the hearing on March 22 with a few remarks about auto safety before calling Ralph Nader as the committee's first witness. But Nader didn't appear.

A murmur ran through the gathering when he didn't emerge from the crowd. Where was he?

Ribicoff then called a 15-minute recess in anticipation of Nader's arrival. When Nader still did not show up, he called his next witness, James Roche, the president of General Motors (at the time one of the world's largest corporations). Roche, in his sixties and wearing a grave expression, was then sworn in to testify under oath, raising his hand as the bank of bright camera lights bathed his every move.

Shortly after Roche began his statement, a number of cameras suddenly swung away to focus on a tall, lanky man with curly black hair who had entered the room. Nader had arrived. After a new round of murmurs died down, the cameras returned to Roche. He continued his remarks by apologizing to Nader.

"I am not here to excuse, condone or justify in any way our investigating Mr. Nader," Roche said. "To the extent that General Motors bears responsibility, I want to apologize here and now to members of this subcommittee and Mr. Nader."

Nader watched as the president of one of the world's most powerful corporations went on to talk about detectives and other investigative matters. However, Roche qualified his comments. He never actually admitted that any harassment occurred. This angered members of the committee.

Senator Robert Kennedy repeatedly grilled Roche about a vaguely written statement that General Motors had released two weeks before. In essence, the statement tried to deny that any harassment had taken place. Ribicoff also jumped in.

"They [the detectives]...ask questions whether a man like Ralph Nader was anti-Semitic. They ask questions about his sex habits," Ribicoff said. "...Before you know it, you have a man who has led a private and honorable life having reflections cast upon his entire character, and that of his family, because of these questions."

Later in the hearing, with one of the detectives testifying, Kennedy said sternly, "This was a form of harassment. What disturbs me even more is that you don't seem to have realized it."

And later, in response to testimony that the investigation had been fair to Nader, Kennedy nearly shouted, "What the hell is all this 'fairness to Ralph'? You keep proving he is not anti-Semitic and he is not [homosexual]. In 'fairness to Ralph'?"

When Nader addressed the committee, he explained his tardiness with a note of humor. "I usually take no more than 12 minutes to come down from my residence to the Capitol by cab," he told the senators and the gathered audience. "And I waited and waited and waited and waited to get a cab, and as my frustration mounted, I almost felt like going out and buying a Chevrolet."

Nader went on to discuss his effort to research and write *Unsafe at Any Speed.* He said he had come across great reluctance and even fear in people involved in the automobile industry. They were afraid to speak out publicly, Nader said, even though they were aware of neglect on the part of the industry when it came to designing safer automobiles.

He realized that the workers' fears of voicing their concerns had led to little or no safety improvements in automobiles over many years. And the price society was paying for this reluctance – thousands of deaths, injuries and grieving families – was great.

Later in his testimony, Senator Kennedy asked Nader straight out, "Why are you doing all this, Mr. Nader?"

"If I were engaged in activities for the prevention of cruelty to animals, nobody would ever ask me that question," Nader responded, in part. "But because I happen…to engage in activities for the prevention of cruelty to humans, my motivations are constantly questioned. When I see people decapitated, crushed, bloodied and broken – and that is really what we're talking about in auto safety, the fatalities and the horrible carnage – I ask myself what the genius of man can do to avoid it."

In confronting General Motors and its investigation, Nader told the senators, "I am responsible for my actions, but who is responsible for those of General Motors? An individual's capital [value] is basically his integrity. He can lose it only once. A corporation can lose its integrity many times and not be affected."

Nader added that individual citizens must be protected from such invasions by corporations, particularly ones so pointedly aimed at destroying a person's character and good name.

"Surely the questioning by private detectives of people who know

Documents in hand, Ralph Nader takes a quick break in 1970 on the steps of the U.S. Capitol Building.

and have worked with me...in an attempt to obtain lurid details and grist for slurs and slanders...becomes an encroachment," he said.

On the evening that Nader reached a monetary settlement with General Motors in 1970 over its investigation, his face was beamed across the nation. The story of the settlement was the lead story that night on ABC, NBC and CBS network news. The following morning, Nader's face graced the front pages of many of the nation's newspapers.

His work for auto safety and General Motors' cruel tactics made Nader's name widely known nationwide. That name recognition has since traveled on with him for more than three decades. Nader's historic battle with General Motors was a tale of an individual citizen taking on a giant corporation with all its vast powers.

It cemented his name with the American public as a David figure who took on a Goliath and won.

A corporation's power had been successfully challenged by a private citizen, in many people's eyes for the first time ever in America. The settlement and resulting victory marked an astounding achievement.

"The best thing about it," Nader says today, "was that it provided momentum for the eventual passage of auto-safety legislation. And that provided a great sense of accomplishment."

Nader took his popularity and widespread name recognition, along with the money from his General Motors' settlement, and worked to make people's lives safer on many fronts. He stated publicly at the time that the money would be "devoted to the cause of safety for all." He has held true to his word.

When you slip on a seat belt, thank Ralph Nader. When you are cradled by an air bag after a car crash, thank Ralph Nader. When you don't breathe cigarette smoke on airline flights, thank Ralph Nader. When the food you eat does not make you sick, thank Ralph Nader. And the list goes on and on.

Much, if not all, of Nader's work revolves around the principles of democracy – government by the people with equal rights and privileges for all. His work is centered around the idea of returning power to common people. He works to shift power away from the corporations and special interests that he believes rule too many parts of people's lives and government today.

Some speakers introduce Ralph Nader by saying, "This man saved my life." This is not a statement you would generally equate with someone working rather calmly on serious matters such as social justice and the environment. However, Nader has devoted his life to saving lives – countless lives. Considering all he has accomplished over the years, the statement rings true.

Chapter Three

Lebanon

A crowd of people talked and laughed in a small house in the town of Zahle, Lebanon. Their voices bounced off of the white walls and tiled floors as they awaited a special guest.

Children dashed between the adults, racing over brightly colored rugs that covered portions of the floor. Kerosene lamps sent light and shadows flickering about the room.

Everyone grew quiet when the visitor arrived. He entered the room in flowing robes, ducking through the doorway to avoid knocking off his tall ornate hat. An archbishop of the Eastern Orthodox Church was paying a visit to the house – quite an honor, especially for a family visiting from America.

After introductions, the archbishop moved slowly around the room. He stopped in front of every person. Each bent and kissed the archbishop's ring – until he came to a small four-year-old boy, who looked up at the archbishop and shook his head.

"I don't have to kiss your ring," the boy said.

And with that, Ralph Nader – already feeling his place in the world – questioned authority for perhaps the first time in his life. It was a stunning statement of defiance for such a small child.

But the archbishop, not upset at all, turned to Ralph's mother and said, "Something is going to come from this young man."

Ralph also had displayed his boldness and bravery on the long trip by ship from the United States. One evening, the ship's constant rocking motion made his sister, Laura, seasick. She stayed in the room while the rest of the family went to dinner.

One of the ship's officers had become fond of the seven-year-old girl. He came by the Naders' table and asked about Laura. When told she was sick, he said he would stop by the family's room to check on her.

Young Ralph had heard enough. He slid off his chair and took off in a dash toward the room. His mother, Rose, called after him and when Ralph didn't stop, chased him. The stunned ship's officer ran after Rose.

"They found Ralph standing in front of the door, with his arms spread across it," says Claire Nader, Ralph's other sister. "He told the man he couldn't go in. He wanted to protect Laura."

The Nader family stayed in Lebanon and lived with Rose's parents for about eight months. During that time, Ralph learned to speak Arabic.

When he came back to the United States, his parents had to argue with local school officials to allow him to attend first grade. The school principal didn't want Ralph to start first grade a year early. But his parents prevailed. And as they suspected, Ralph had no problems in school.

The Nader family had traveled to Lebanon in 1937 for a visit. Rose and her husband, Nathra, Ralph's father, wanted to show their children the Middle Eastern country of their birth, and introduce them to the culture and their grandparents.

"We were taught to be proud of Lebanon, proud of where our parents came from," Claire says. "We were taught that people from

With his sister Laura at his side, Ralph Nader poses for a photo as a young child.

other countries had something to offer and bring to America. There wasn't a rush, as we grew up, to leave our Lebanese culture behind."

Rose Nader's parents raised eight daughters, two nieces and two nephews under one roof in Zahle, a town set amidst vineyards in the hills above Lebanon's Bekkaa Valley.

Nathra, a few years older than Rose, came from the mountain village of Arsoun.

Rose's mother made almost everything for her family from scratch, including clothes and wool-stuffed mattresses. Rose helped her mother bake bread in a mud brick oven, which was set apart from the house.

During most of Rose's years in Lebanon, the Ottoman Empire of the Turks ruled the country. Starting in 1914, World War I brought hard times, including food shortages, disease epidemics and military occupations. Turkish soldiers often wandered through Rose's neighborhood. After the war ended in 1918, Turkish rule was replaced by French rule.

Ralph's father, Nathra, first came to the United States in 1912. Nathra had grown tired of a lack of freedom in his country, tired of its undemocratic system. He decided to leave even though he had very little money. "When your enemy is your judge, who do you complain to?" he used to ask, speaking of both the French and Turkish rulers of Lebanon.

Nathra loved the freedom he found in America. As he floated past the Statue of Liberty, arriving in New York City on a huge ship, the experience moved him. "When I passed by the Statue of Liberty, I took it seriously," he liked to say.

He worked a number of jobs along the East Coast and saved his money. He then returned to Lebanon in 1925, where he met and married Rose. The couple immigrated to the United States and settled in Danbury, Connecticut.

A year later they moved about an hour north to a small town at the confluence of the Mad and Still rivers, set in the foothills of the Berkshire Mountains. There, in Winsted, Connecticut, they opened a restaurant and started a family.

The Naders first had a son, Shafeek, then daughters Claire and Laura. Ralph became the baby of the family, born Feb. 27, 1934.

Chapter Four

Winsted, Connecticut

When most little boys his age were still kicking around notions of being firefighters, policemen or even super heroes, Ralph Nader already knew what he wanted to be – a lawyer. An unusual choice for a young child, to be sure.

Several times when he was just five and six years old, Ralph visited the county courthouse in his hometown of Winsted, Connecticut. He sat in the back of the courtroom with his father and watched as lawyers presented their cases, judges made rulings and juries delivered verdicts. The courtroom and its proceedings fascinated him.

"I wanted to be a lawyer from a very early age. There was never much discussion of anything else," Ralph says. "The way I saw it, lawyers fought for justice, fought for the underdogs, took on the big guys. That suited me just fine."

Part of Ralph's early love of law and the legal system came from his father. Nathra often had business at the courthouse and town hall. He wasn't shy about going to court to fight for causes he believed in, to fight for his rights.

One time, when the telephone company decided to charge him rent for a pay phone at the family's restaurant, Nathra brought the matter to court. "They are using my place of business to make money," Nathra explained to the judge. "Why do they need to charge me on top of that?"

"My father would go to court on his own, and he knew how to argue," Ralph says. "He could usually persuade the judge."

Nathra believed the legal system laid the groundwork for people's rights and responsibilities. It also provided a way to make positive changes in society. He believed lawyers could help bring justice to discouraged citizens and that the legal profession was one of the world's most powerful.

"From my father, I learned early on that the legal profession was flexible and could provide an exciting place from which to try to improve society," Ralph says. "I also learned that it could provide a safeguard for our democracy."

Of course, Ralph also was "just a kid." He liked to do lots of things besides visiting the courthouse. He played marbles with his sisters. He climbed the giant maple tree in front of his house. He rode his bike all over town.

The Nader house sat on a hill above downtown Winsted. A handful of fruit trees were scattered in the yard around the white, 10-room house. In front of the house, a canopy of trees shaded the street from either side, their branches meeting over the narrow road.

The Nader children remember a relaxed and simple life while growing up in Winsted. They played in clubhouses of blankets and boxes that they built in both the attic and basement. Life didn't seem as rushed as it does today, Claire says. Her parents didn't drive the children all over town to various activities.

"Our mother believed that children needed a quiet space around them so they could just do what they wanted at certain times," she says. "At those times, our activities were what we created."

One favorite spot of the Nader children seemed to rise up to the sky on top of the hill behind their house. It was a 60-foot-tall stone monument built to honor soldiers who died in the Civil War. On special occasions in the summer, the four children took their lunches up to the monument, each sitting on the cool stone of an archway leading to the monument.

"You'd get up and look at it every morning," Ralph says. "It was beautiful and meant a lot to us. It had old cannons around it to play on, and we'd play football up by it. It also was a great place to fly kites. You could let them run out a thousand feet, flying them way out over the woods and town."

The town of Winsted in the 1930s and 1940s revolved around the operations of about 30 small factories. In 1898, the number had been nearly 100. The Waring Company first made its kitchen blenders in Winsted, and the famous Gilbert Clock Company made clocks by the thousands.

When Ralph was growing up, a lot of the small factories made textiles, or cloth, while others made sewing pins and various types of electrical equipment. Winsted, like many other New England towns at the time, was known as a "mill town" due to all of the manufacturing activity. Nonetheless, it remained a pleasant, quiet small town of about 10,000 residents.

The town meant a lot to Rose and Nathra. To them, just as important as being good parents was the need to be good citizens.

"They were concerned people and had a deep interest in public matters," Ralph says. "They gave us a sense that it was important to be a citizen – that you had civic responsibilities."

Many times, the dinner table at the Nader house provided a forum for discussing civic responsibilities, along with a host of other subjects. In fact, the Nader family's dinners have become sort of famous over the years.

During World War II in the 1940s, "victory gardens" tended by American homeowners helped increase U.S. food production. Here, a nine-year-old Ralph Nader (right) and one of his friends show off some fresh produce grown in a home garden in Winsted, Conn.

"Dad was not for much small talk at the dinner table," Laura says. "He read newspapers and knew about the problems of pollution, politics and workers' rights. He posed social problems for the family to talk about, asking, 'What do you think we should do about…whatever? Is it right that …?' And we'd be off in a discussion."

On many occasions, the discussions were lengthy. Dinner at the Nader house lasted for hours some nights. Everyone took part, no matter their age. Everyone contributed their opinions.

"There were some unspoken rules," Claire says. "You had to stand your ground. You couldn't just throw up your hands and say,

'Oh well.' You were encouraged to say why you believed what you did, or explain why you were irritated or upset.

"It was very stimulating," she adds. "Going to school was nothing compared to being at our dinner table."

On many occasions, Ralph provided a laugh or two at the family dinner table. Still today, his sisters speak fondly of his sense of humor. "He was always playing on words and getting us to laugh," Laura says.

Although this argumentative dinner scene might sound harsh to some people, the Naders thrived on it. Laura thinks her family's dinner discussions started Ralph on the path he eventually followed.

Of course, Ralph's mother Rose also played a big role in how he and his siblings would go on to lead their lives. Rose always told her children that "determination puts your dreams on wheels." Following his mother's advice, Ralph made determination one of his trademarks.

Chapter Five

Boyhood

"Y ou want to go for a ride?" Ralph's father asked one afternoon, as he would on occasion.

"Sure," responded the then 10-year-old Ralph.

The two piled in the family car and took off. Ralph had no idea where they were headed. Soon they came to the local hospital.

"You know how that hospital was built?" his father asked.

"No," came the answer.

"In 1900, a wealthy person in this town donated $10,000," Nathra said. "It became the first hospital in the county."

The pair traveled up around a bend and drove by the impressive brick building housing the Gilbert Home for Orphans. Same question from Nathra. Same response from Ralph.

"A local company donated money to build it – the Gilbert Clock Company," he said.

Around another corner they came across the Gilbert School. Same thing: Gilbert Clock Company money given to the community to build a prominent high school.

Finally, they swung by the Beardsley and Memorial Library.

"In 1902, a woman named Beardsley gave $10,000 of her money to build that library," Nathra said. "You know, in the last 40 years more than 100 people in this town have had that kind of money.

Can you imagine what kind of place this would be if they had each given a gift like that?

"The wealth of a nation is about people, not dollars," he told Ralph later as they pulled into the driveway. "If you want a rich nation, you have to love and help each other."

A longtime Nader friend, David Halberstam, remembers Ralph's father well. Halberstam, who won a prestigious Pulitzer Prize for his writing about the Vietnam War, spent the fourth through eighth grades with Ralph. They have remained friends over the years.

"Ralph's father took great pleasure in being free in this country. He had a real zest for it," Halberstam says. "He was very grateful for the freedoms he found here and was a wonderful democrat – with a lowercase 'd.'" (As in the political system, not the Democratic Party.)

"He knew you could stand up for your rights in America and believe in the things that Lincoln, Jefferson and Washington put down on paper," he says. "You were supposed to use your voice to do something for this great gift of freedom. Like his father, Ralph has a great and intense feel for America. America as it was meant to be."

Nathra Nader let his zest for freedom shine nearly every day in his place of business, the Highland Arms Restaurant. Nathra and Rose owned the restaurant-bakery on Main Street. Nathra ran the business while Rose focused on the couple's home and children. The name came from the region – the "highlands" of northwestern Connecticut – and the idea of "arms" reaching out to embrace the community.

All kinds of people visited the restaurant – mill workers,

Bundled up for a winter day in New England, Ralph Nader, about 11 years old, stops for a snapshot in his hometown of Winsted, Conn.

tourists, traveling salespeople and jurors from the courthouse down the street. Others showed up without money. Nonetheless, the Naders took care of everyone who showed up hungry at the restaurant, asking for food, Claire said. (And during the Great Depression in the 1930s, there were plenty of people in need.)

As Ralph grew up and worked all the various jobs at the business, he met and talked to many of the customers. Running the cash register and waiting tables were his favorite jobs because they allowed him time to visit with people.

"The whistle would blow, and the workers would come pouring out of the mills," Ralph says. "I talked to them all and learned from them all. I'd ask about what they were doing, what they knew. I learned a lot more from them than they did from me."

Ralph's father also liked dealing with his customers, but he didn't listen as much as his son. Nathra liked to express his ideas and thoughts – sometimes whether the customers liked it or not. People in Winsted liked to say, "For a nickel, you got a cup of coffee and a conversation."

"Talking with people was the thing my father enjoyed most about his business," Laura says. "You couldn't get out of the place without talking to him. When he rang up customers at the register, he would hold their change in his hand and then address some political or social problem – all the time with a little smile on his face."

Halberstam remembers visiting the restaurant with his uncle on many early mornings before they took off fishing. It was the only place open that early. He recalls Nathra as "hard working and, in a wonderful way, argumentative."

When things went wrong in the restaurant, Ralph was a blessing to have around. He could get customers to laugh when orders got mixed up or the kitchen was slow. "He'd use his sense of humor to keep people occupied, while he worked at the same time to correct the mistake," his sister Claire says. "The restaurant work provided Ralph with a great education."

Igor Stravinsky

Chapter Six

6

"I think I'm going to throw up," 14-year-old Ralph thought to himself. "I'm not going to be able to do this."

He sat in the living room, very nervous, his stomach a mess. In a couple of hours he had to give a speech in front of a large auditorium full of people. His speech – on the famous naturalist John Muir who helped create California's Yosemite National Park – would allow him to finish the eighth grade.

Although he had spent hours and hours researching and memorizing the 10-minute speech, the whole experience now terrified him. "This will be the worst 10 minutes of my life," he thought, "if I live through it."

About this time, his brother walked into the room. Shafeek noticed his pale-white little brother.

"What's wrong?" he asked. "You look terrible."

"I don't think I can remember my speech," Ralph mumbled. "I'm very nervous."

"You know who Igor Stravinsky is, right?" he asked.

"Yeah. What's that got to do with it?" Ralph responded, a little upset that his brother was asking him about a famous composer of music at a time like this.

Shafeek then told Ralph the story of Stravinsky's "The Rite of

Spring." The story goes something like this:

Stravinsky's newest work premiered in Paris, France, in 1913. But it was very different from anything he had produced before. Different from anything any musical composer had done before, for that matter. It broke tradition by being forceful, pounding and primitive.

Right after the orchestra began playing the music, people in the audience started laughing sarcastically. A few minutes later, they were downright mad. Soon a general uproar filled the theater, caused by the enraged audience. Some people whistled or hollered or booed at the stage. Others stood up and left.

Stravinsky fled the scene in embarrassment. The affair became known as one of the most wild and bizarre musical performances of the twentieth century. But as with many new things, "The Rite of Spring" is now known as one of the most famous and respected compositions in modern musical literature.

"Can you imagine how Stravinsky felt that night – what he went through?" Shafeek said. "Now let's consider what you face with your speech. You're going to a place where everyone loves students. Even if you completely blow it, no one is going to walk out, no one is going to stand up and shout. What you have to go through is pretty simple in comparison. What are you worried about?"

Although Shafeek's story helped a little bit, it didn't completely take care of Ralph's stage fright. Just before his turn, Claire remembers worrying about her brother. He sat with his head down, staring at his lap.

"But when the time came, his voice was as clear as a bell, and he delivered the speech beautifully," Claire says. "Afterward, he talked about how he could've presented it better. And he still waits the same way today before he speaks – head down, looking at his lap."

Shafeek's Stravinsky story did end up helping Ralph in the long run, however.

"Shafeek gave me another frame of reference to consider," Ralph says. "After that speech, I honestly was never again afraid to speak in public."

Shafeek, who died in 1986, meant a lot to Ralph and his sisters throughout their lives. They all agree that he was a perfect big brother.

Being the oldest, Shafeek played the role of cultural translator between the parents in their new surroundings in America and the younger children. For Ralph, Shafeek also played the role of a second father because of the eight-year difference in their ages.

Shafeek loved books and reading. He shared that love with his siblings. He even made lists of books for his little brother to read, which Ralph did. Ralph posted the list on the inside of his closet door. The two brothers would then discuss the books.

Like his parents, Shafeek also took his role as a citizen seriously. He attended many town meetings – a New England tradition in which residents meet and hash out decisions for their communities in sometimes-fiery, give-and-take arguments.

"He had an incredible civic imagination," Ralph says. "I've never seen anyone argue so effectively."

The best example of Shafeek's civic mindedness is the Northwestern Connecticut Community College in Winsted. It exists because of his hard-fought, all-volunteer effort to make the school a reality.

"He had read a lot about community colleges," Ralph says of his brother. "And because of that, he could fend off the people who said that it couldn't be done."

When the Gilbert School (the town's high school, from which Ralph graduated in 1951) moved to a new building, Shafeek decided a community college should be started up in the vacated building.

Shafeek worked hard on a plan to create a private community college, which went on to become Connecticut's first community college in its newly established system.

With all these citizenship-based activities in the Nader family, it's no wonder that some of the things Ralph liked to do were considered rather strange for kids his age. A year after his John Muir speech, at age 14, Ralph fell in love with the *Congressional Record*. He came across a pile of them in a closet at the school library and couldn't put them down.

The *Congressional Record* is the printed publication of the proceedings of the U.S. Congress, including transcripts of all the various discussions. The government publishes it daily while Congress is in session.

"It was my first introduction to Congress, and it got me into it right away," Ralph says. "I was fascinated by the different senators and representatives, and what they said in the *Record*. Some were constantly anticommunist and others always in favor of big business, while other members just liked to note the anniversaries of places and people in their districts and states."

Though the *Record* is not your typical reading material for a teenager, Ralph loved it. But just as when he was a little boy, he liked to do lots of ordinary things, too. He ran one of the biggest paper routes in town. He played a lot of sandlot baseball and became a big fan of professional baseball.

Some mornings as a teenager, Ralph would get up very early and catch a train to New York City to watch an afternoon Yankees game. A return train would get him back to Winsted that evening.

One of Ralph's fondest memories of childhood involves – of all things – leaves. Every fall Ralph's family and people around town raked big piles of leaves into the street's gutters. When the heat of the day subsided and a setting sun left a cool autumn evening to enjoy, they would light the piles of leaves on fire.

The flames from the crackling and burning leaves gave the neighborhood a soft orange glow and created a glorious fall evening, Ralph remembers. As darkness fell, smoke curled up through now-empty branches hanging over the street and disappeared into a thin blue sky.

In the fall of 1951, however, Ralph wasn't around to rake leaves at his parents' house in Winsted. He had been accepted to Princeton University and now attended college in New Jersey.

Chapter Seven

Princeton

Dead birds. As Ralph Nader walked under the trees, he noticed dead birds.

And not just one or two. There were more than a dozen of them spread around the ground under the trees and on the sidewalk. What was going on?

Nader knew someone regularly sprayed pesticides to kill insects on the trees at Princeton University, where he was then a student. He had watched men in trucks with big tanks of liquid chemicals pull out huge hoses and shoot streams of spray up at the trees.

"Sometimes students were sprayed going to and from classes," Nader says. "I remember getting sprayed with the stuff myself."

But what about the birds?

"They weren't mutilated," he says. "It was pretty easy to put things together and conclude that their deaths probably were caused by the spray, which I knew contained the chemical DDT. I decided to take a couple of the birds up to the school newspaper to let them know they should look into it."

When Nader arrived, he found a reporter on the paper leaning back in his chair with his feet propped up on his desk. The reporter was not interested when Nader showed him the dead birds and told him of his discovery. In fact, he acted bothered by Nader's intrusion into his office.

"Listen," he bluntly informed Nader. "We have some of the best chemistry and biology professors in the nation here. They're smart, all right? If there was a problem with DDT, don't you think they would've figured it out?"

"Look what it's obviously done to these birds," Nader replied. "You don't think it might be harmful to people, too?"

After the reporter waved him off, Nader wrote a letter to the editor for publication in the school newspaper. But the editor refused to run the letter, even after Nader went back and argued with him.

"I learned then that you can have very smart people around, but if they are not interested in finding out what might be going on – or are simply busy with their own research or consulting – things can get missed. Important things," Nader says. "It was a perfect example of what people will take for granted if they've been conditioned to trust the system."

Ten years later, a woman named Rachel Carson wrote a famous book called *Silent Spring*. In it she correctly claimed that the pesticide DDT posed a huge danger to animals and possibly humans. The chemical nearly wiped out several bird species. DDT has been banned in the United States since 1972, although it is still used in other parts of the world.

Although Nader enjoyed his studies at Princeton, he grew tired of the "gentleman C" mentality at the school. Many students came from rich and connected families with businesses and wealth to support them after they finished college. Some of them decided they didn't need to study too hard. They worked just hard enough to get passing "C" grades, and then moved on in life.

That attitude made Nader think back to something his father

had told him. "Colleges can teach you how to make a living," Nathra said. "But they can't teach you how to live a life."

Nader studied hard. He even "audited" extra classes, simply to learn more. That meant he attended classes that he hadn't signed up for – just to listen to teachers' lectures, but not to take tests or write papers. He loved to learn. But he had to put up with plenty of name-calling because of it.

"If you studied hard, you were known as a 'grind,'" Nader says. "I remember being on the ground floor of the library with the windows open. Guys would come by in the evening and jeer at me. 'Dirty grind,' they'd call out. Being caught in the library was a bad thing, if you can imagine."

The name-calling – along with his undying desire to learn – eventually led Nader to begin slipping through an open window at night to study in another building on campus. One night a professor caught him sneaking through the window. When Nader explained his intent, the teacher got him an extra key to the building.

Nader also grew tired of the way young men dressed at Princeton University. Everyone wore the same thing – white shirts, khaki pants and white-buck shoes. It was so boring, Nader thought. One day, to show his disgust with the sheep-like, everyone-wear-the-same-thing mentality, he went to class in a bathrobe and slippers.

Hitchhiking became a Nader trademark and a valued way to get around while at Princeton. The practice of sticking your thumb out and hitching rides on New Jersey's Route One was not commonplace in the early 1950s, but Nader loved the adventure it provided. And like working at his father's restaurant, hitchhiking provided him another way to talk to all kinds of people, listen to their stories and learn from their experiences.

Built in 1897, East Pyne Hall on the Princeton University campus today is used for offices and classrooms for the school's literature departments. Nader graduated from Princeton in 1955.

"I never took a bus or train out of Princeton the whole time I was there, except maybe once," he remembers. "By hitchhiking, I met all kinds of people – everyone from doctors to truck drivers. It was one of the greatest educations in the world."

Truck drivers complained to Nader about their rigs' cramped spaces, which they were forced to sit in day after day in great discomfort. Nader noticed that in many trucks, a metal coat hanger stuck out from the wall of the cab, right behind the drivers' heads. Not a wise spot, he thought, if they were in an accident and their heads were thrown backward.

The drivers also told Nader about the many close calls they had, in terms of traffic accidents barely avoided for any number of reasons. Along with those stories, Ralph saw plenty of accidents first hand.

"I hitchhiked so much – we're talking tens of thousands of miles – that on a number of occasions, we were the first on the scene of traffic accidents," he says. "I saw lots of terrible sights, lots of trauma. And I began to examine the crashes closely, noticing how the cars were bent out of shape and how the people had been injured by being thrown out of vehicles or burned in car fires."

Many of these crashes were along the infamous Route One, a major highway that ran north from Princeton to New York City. Although it was a divided highway, it was not what we know today as an "interstate highway." Hundreds of side roads crossed Route One , and lots of traffic constantly hopped on and off the highway. Accidents happened often.

All these crashes and injuries, as well as the unsafe traffic patterns on Route One and other roadways, got Nader to thinking. It would be a subject he would look into further at his next educational stop.

But first Nader had some traveling to do. The summer before

his senior year at Princeton, he returned to Lebanon. He studied the nation's agricultural development for his senior thesis and visited many of his relatives. This trip got him thinking about more travel. As soon as he graduated from Princeton, finishing in the top 10 percent of his class, he caught a ride with a medical student all the way across the country.

Nader visited Native American Indian reservations in Arizona, New Mexico and Montana. The terrible poverty and rough living conditions shocked him. The mental state of many Native Americans, who felt hopeless in fighting the U.S. government for their rights, also troubled him.

He talked to various people on the reservations and eventually wrote a long article on the harsh conditions faced by many American Indians, noting their high rates of alcoholism and suicide. It became his first major published article and eventually thousands of copies were printed by an organization working to improve Native American living conditions.

Nader ended up in California's Yosemite National Park in California that summer. He worked in the park's grocery store. On his way back to the East Coast, news flashed of a terrible flood in northern Connecticut. When Nader couldn't get through on the phone to his parents, he immediately headed home.

The flood destroyed half of downtown Winsted, carrying debris from half of its buildings downriver late one night. Being on the side of Main Street farthest from the river, the family's Highland Arms Restaurant made it through the flood – although it sustained heavy damage. Five feet of floodwaters flowed through its interior. Ralph helped his family clean up the mess. The restaurant eventually reopened for business, and Ralph headed off to Harvard Law School in the fall of 1955.

Harvard Law

H itchhiking again. Nader and the man who had given him a ride traveled down a stretch of road between Hartford, the capital of Connecticut, and Boston, the capital of Massachusetts. They talked about nothing in particular. This had become a familiar route to Nader as he traveled between his home in Connecticut and his classes at Harvard Law School.

Suddenly, ahead of them and off to the side of the road, they spotted a jumble of cars. Several were mangled from the impact of slamming into each other. Others sat at strange angles from the road, smoke pouring from their hoods. No ambulances, no police cars. Nader and his traveling companion were the first on the accident scene.

Nader walked over to one of the wrecked cars to see if anyone was hurt. He saw what no one should ever have to see. The scene always will be with him. A small girl riding in the front seat of the car lay dead. The force of the crash had thrown her toward the dashboard. As her tiny body flew forward, the small door of the car's glove compartment came down. It cut off her head.

"It was gruesome, as you can imagine," Nader says. He still shakes his head with sadness as he thinks back to the horrific sight. "The glove-box door worked just like a guillotine on that little girl. That got me to begin looking more seriously at the issue of auto safety."

That more serious look at car safety would come late in Nader's stint at Harvard Law School. Most of his three years at the school were marked with disillusionment, an uneasiness with the place and its teaching style that he could never shake. For one thing, Harvard sits in the midst of Cambridge, next to Boston. Although he found city life a little unsettling, the school itself caused most of his unrest.

"I didn't like Harvard Law all that much," Nader says. "There was no life in the law they taught there. It was ridiculously narrow – all designed to support commercial law firms and corporations. Law for the rich."

Nader often wondered why there was no study of environmental law, civil rights law or law that dealt with other social issues. Where was the law for the people, not just corporations? That kind of law wasn't happening in the 1950s at Harvard Law, one of the nation's most prestigious schools.

"It was basically a high-priced factory," he says. "But instead of producing toasters or blenders, they were producing lawyers to serve corporations, and that was it."

Unlike Princeton, everyone studied very hard at the law school. Unfortunately, Nader learned that most of the students studied hard so they could go out and make lots of money. For many, fame and money would mark their success. Nader wanted his success to be based on the idea of public service.

Bucking a trend once again, Nader decided he didn't want to study so conventionally this time around. He skipped classes. Although he usually scored well enough on tests, he didn't study much before exams and continued to audit classes. It was his way of protesting the way the school prepared its students to be lawyers.

Once in a while, Nader took off from school and left town.

During a crucial period of his third and final year of law school, he got word that his sister was sick. He went to Mexico to visit Laura, who was doing anthropology work outside the city of Oaxaca.

"I was way up in the mountains," Laura says. "It took 20 hours by truck and foot to reach my very isolated village from Oaxaca. But Ralph made it. I was sick with malaria, and he came to give me encouragement and support."

The closest Nader came to a positive experience at law school involved the student newspaper, the *Harvard Law School Record*. He became interested in journalistic writing and had many articles published during the three years he worked for the paper. His piece about conditions on the Indian reservations was first published in the *Record*.

When Nader was elected president of the paper during his second year of law school, he proposed turning the *Record* into a publication with a national presence, a more ambitious scope. The paper's governing board, however, narrowly voted down his idea. Nader resigned as president, but stayed on as a writer.

He decided to write about automobile safety at one point in his senior year and had an article published, titled "American Cars: Designed for Death." This journalism experience soon would come in handy, as he was about to start writing stories from the road – and author an important book.

But first, after graduating from Harvard Law School in 1958, Nader faced a short stint in the Army. A military draft existed for young men at the time, and Nader chose to join the Army Reserves. In doing so, he signed up for eight weeks of grueling basic training and four months of full-time duty, followed by

During a trip to South America in 1963, Nader wrote a series of articles for several American magazines. On his trip, he visited a number of Latin America's great cities, including Quito, the capital of Ecuador. Pictured above is one of the city's outdoor markets, where all kinds of fresh fruits and vegetables are sold.

inactive reserve service for the next few years. He ended up at Fort Dix in New Jersey.

"I liked the Army Reserves," Nader says. "If you want to know a little bit about what the military is like, it's a priceless experience."

During basic training, each man was taught a skill. Nader became a cook and learned to make all kinds of food in an Army kitchen. This suited him fine, since he loved to eat and was impressed with the quality of food the Army bought.

"I loved Army food," he says. "At that time, it was all made from scratch and was very wholesome. Fresh fruit, vegetables, meat and big pots of soup – and I had an enormous appetite from all the physical activity we undertook."

Nader also enjoyed learning how mess sergeants cooked meals for thousands of men. He remembers one morning when he rose early and with other bakers successfully made banana bread for thousands of soldiers. He also remembers having fun with the guys in the serving line and guessing what food they would choose.

"It was a kick," he says. "They all had certain preferences, and we would start trying to guess their choices."

Nader liked the cooking portion of his Army duties, but he could have done without all the typing he faced at night.

"Once they found out I was a Harvard Law School graduate, that was it for me. I faced double duty," Nader recalls. "My superiors had me typing files most nights at company headquarters."

When he got out of the Army, Nader entered a five-year period in which he pursued different topics, but always stayed with his auto-safety research and writing. He worked some law-related jobs, taught some college courses and wrote some freelance magazine articles. He also took several long trips outside the country. Two in particular stand out.

Nader took a trip to Scandinavia in 1961 to study the region's ombudsman system. An ombudsman is an official who investigates complaints by citizens against government agencies. Nader liked the idea. It provided a way for individual citizens to resolve their disputes with government. He hoped he could make the idea work in America.

Using his own money, he traveled to Denmark, Norway, Sweden and Finland, and met with each country's ombudsman. The ombudsmen and their staffs were an arm of the parliamentary government who worked with citizens, but also released published criticisms of various government agencies and operations. They served as watchdogs to keep the government in line.

Although Nader believes he first introduced the European system to the United States, the ombudsman idea did not take off, despite his efforts. A bill Nader helped draft was introduced in the Connecticut legislature, but it failed to become law. However, the idea did catch on in California and Hawaii for a while.

While in Scandinavia, Nader took a two-week side trip to the Soviet Union and wrote several articles for American magazines. At one point, he broke away from his tour guide in Moscow and made his way to the offices of *Krokodil* magazine. The publication was famous for its humorous and satirical stories on Russian society.

"I walked in the back door, and the guys there were reading *Time* magazine," Nader says. "They knew plenty about America, asking me about professional basketball players and [the author] Truman Capote."

Nader later ventured south to Latin America in 1963. Before he left, he made arrangements to send a series of articles to *The Christian Science Monitor* and the *National Observer*, which he hoped would pay for his travels. Nader and a friend left for South America in June and visited Venezuela, Brazil, Uruguay, Argentina, Chile, Peru, Ecuador and Colombia on a grand three-month trip.

Nader visited with and interviewed hundreds of people during the journey. Sometimes his probing questions made them mad, but they gave him plenty of story material. He wrote 30 articles from the information he gathered.

"In Peru, one banker admitted to him that, 'These people don't have a chance. We've got them by the neck [referring to his fellow citizens],'" Ralph's sister Claire says. "Ralph's travels stimulated him and allowed him to see the contrasts between the powerful and poor."

On his South American journey, Nader also realized that the world was connected. He watched kids all over the world enjoying the same songs. And he witnessed American companies running operations all over the globe – another contrast of the powerful and the poor.

About a year later, Nader sought out his childhood friend David Halberstam, who now worked as a reporter for *The New York Times*. Halberstam had won the Pulitzer Prize in 1964 for his early reports from the Vietnam War, and Nader wanted to visit with him. They met in a restaurant in Washington, D.C., but Halberstam came to the lunch meeting wondering about Nader's intentions. His writing about the Vietnam War had angered many people, and Halberstam now didn't know who to trust.

"I'd been beaten up by the U.S. government, and I had all kinds of people after me because of my writing," Halberstam says. "They wanted to know who I had talked to. They wanted to court-martial my anonymous military sources. I had gotten a taste of what Ralph would eventually go through with General Motors."

In fact, one of Halberstam's old college acquaintances already had come around to visit. Halberstam later found out that this acquaintance was searching out information about his sources, not simply catching up with an old friend.

During lunch, the conversation stayed mainly on Halberstam's adventures and reporting work in Vietnam. When talk turned to Nader's activities, Ralph mentioned his trip to South America, as well as his travels in Scandinavia and the Soviet Union. In his typical fashion, however, Nader did not reveal much about other parts of his life. And Nader didn't explain why he had gone to these places, just talked about the people he had met.

This sent alarm bells ringing for Halberstam.

"I thought, 'The same thing is happening to me again. Ralph Nader is working for the CIA,'" Halberstam says today, laughing as he remembers the encounter and his wrong assumption.

A while later, Halberstam returned to his hometown of Winsted to speak to a gathering at the high school and discuss his Pulitzer Prize-winning work. At a party after the event, Halberstam ran into Ralph's father, Nathra.

"He was very excited. He kept telling me, 'It's young people like you and Ralph who will do great things for this country,'" Halberstam says. "I remember thinking, 'Yes, thank you very much, but what is this stuff about Ralph? What has he done?'"

From his recent lunch with him, Halberstam knew Nader hadn't talked of any important plans or work. However, this vague stretch of Nader's life after Harvard was about to end as he entered a new period of clear focus, extreme determination and great success.

Chapter Nine

'Unsafe'

9

R alph Nader squinted through the rain-splattered glass, scanning the airport road outside. He decided to step out into the light rain. At the curb, he set his briefcase down and glanced both ways. Where were they? What were they driving?

He had come to the Detroit airport several times for meetings with auto-industry workers. But these weren't your usual business meetings. They were held in the back seats of cars, as their drivers slowly circled the airport. The subject was auto safety, and it wasn't necessarily safe for people to talk openly about it.

Finally, a car pulled up. Nader looked in, recognized a familiar face and climbed into the back seat. It was time to do more research.

"I had a number of these secret meetings when I was first started looking into auto safety," Nader says. "We'd meet and circle around the airport because people were afraid of hidden microphones. Then I'd fly back home.

"Sometimes I met with engineers, other times with assembly-line workers. All were people who had evidence of systematic defects in the cars they were building but were afraid to talk about them publicly for fear of losing their jobs."

Through aggressive efforts such as these, Nader slowly gathered a body of knowledge on various auto-safety problems. All of his notes and research eventually played a role in his writing of the book, *Unsafe at Any Speed: The Designed-In Dangers of the American Automobile.*

But Nader's first writing on the subject came during his final year of law school at Harvard. He wrote an article for the *Harvard Law Record,* titled "American Cars: Designed for Death." He also wrote a paper for one of his classes on the subject.

After his exploration phase, involving the Army, international travel and miscellaneous law-related work, Nader turned his focus once again to auto safety. He had done some legal work representing people injured in car accidents during those years. Now he decided he would try to prevent injuries before they happened.

Throughout his life, Nader always had great empathy for people who were hurt or in trouble. Those feelings for other people's pain and suffering intensified as he came across accident after accident on the highways.

"When Ralph saw that 50,000 people died in car accidents, he didn't just see a number," says his sister, Laura. "He saw 50,000 individual people."

"He has a profound reaction to people who are hurt," adds his other sister, Claire. "He is able to put himself in other people's pain. He genuinely feels for them."

Nader moved to Washington, D.C., in 1964. He began working for Daniel Patrick Moynihan, the Assistant Secretary of Labor who went on to serve as a senator from New York. Moynihan also was concerned about auto safety and had worked to improve the safety of car and truck tires. Nader's job involved doing research and writing a report on what the federal government could do in terms of highway safety.

Nader spent many late nights working on the report, which ran more than 200 pages when he finished. Moynihan wanted to make it safe politically for President Lyndon Johnson to go against the auto companies and sign into law new auto-safety regulations. Nader's report, he hoped, would help make that possible.

Nader's work on the report, along with his study of the auto-safety issue while at Harvard, put him in a good position to write a book on the subject. He decided to leave his job at the Labor Department after finishing the report and do just that. After a friend introduced Nader to a publisher named Richard Grossman, who wanted to publish such a book, Nader fell on the task with great devotion.

He worked 18 hours a day, seven days a week. Over a six-month period, Nader pored over all of his previous research while he continued to gather more. His book came together quickly, and Grossman wasted no time in publishing the book once it was finished.

"It was exciting because there was a definite deadline I had to meet. There's nothing like writing under a deadline," Nader says. "Then it took just two months to get the book out – unprecedented at the time. If it had taken the usual year from manuscript to hardback book, it would've blown the whole thing. A lot of what ended up happening wouldn't have happened. The book ended up being the bait for the auto companies – the magnet that drew them in."

Unsafe at Any Speed served as bait in part because it took such a hard stand against the auto companies. It accused the industry of choosing style over safety in its search for bigger profits.

In particular, it took to task General Motors' Corvair. Numerous accidents had been occurring with the company's sports car, many of them apparently not involving driver error. Something in

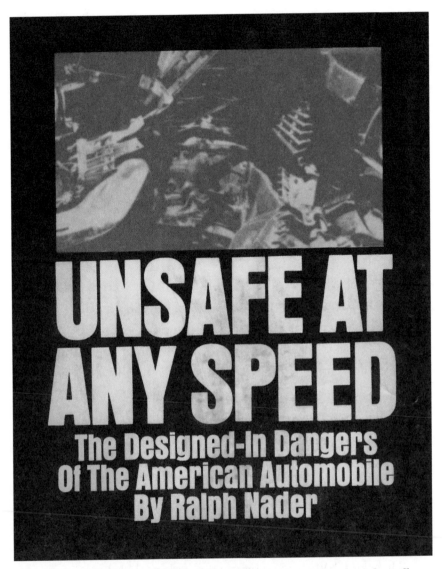

Nader's famous book on auto safety, Unsafe at Any Speed, *became a bestseller not long after it was published in 1965.*

the car's rear suspension system kept going wrong. The problem occasionally sent Corvairs spinning out of control for no reason, many times killing or severely injuring their drivers. Owners even tried keeping different air pressures in the rear tires to avoid the problem. In addition, a rigid steering column acted like a spear in many accidents, impaling drivers.

Nader wrote that General Motors was negligent in letting all of this happen, which at the time was a shocking and unheard-of stance to take against a corporation.

In the book, Nader also looked at simple things, such as fancy ornaments on cars' hoods and tail fins sticking out at the back. These sharp pieces of metal acted as dangerous weapons when cars collided with bike riders or pedestrians. Nader questioned why style elements such as these were taking precedence over safety.

As well, he mentioned the notion of the "second collision" – when people were slammed around the inside of cars after the first impact of an accident. These second collisions, caused by a lack of seat belts in cars, often were more deadly than the initial crash. Nader couldn't forget the passengers he had seen horribly cut up when they flew forward into sharp-edged panels. Lap-only seat belts at the time were not a requirement, just an unpromoted option.

Overall, *Unsafe at Any Speed* stated that the way a car was designed could provide safety for its drivers and passengers in a crash. Oddly enough, few people had seriously considered this before. Nader also made another important connection. If you can't control the way people drive, he figured, why not control the outcome of their actions?

"He asked, 'Why do we have a technology that doesn't consider injuries?'" Laura says. "The brilliance of it was that he separated injuries from accidents. You knew accidents would always happen, but why do you have to have injuries? At amusement parks, protection is provided on bumper cars. Why not in real cars?"

In the very beginning of the book, Nader stated that American

Ralph Nader shakes hands with U.S. President Lyndon Johnson on Sept. 9, 1966. Johnson had just signed the National Traffic and Motor Vehicle Safety Act, which required the auto industry to meet specific safety standards.

society had developed a great system of police, ambulances and hospitals to respond to car accidents. "But the true mark of a humane society must be what it does about the prevention of accident injuries, not just the cleaning up of them afterward," he wrote.

He also pointed out the problems of controlling large companies, which too often ignore the harmful effects of the way they conduct their business. And finally, he criticized the U.S. government for not setting safety standards and passing laws that auto manufacturers had to follow.

These three themes – safety, the power of business and the

responsibility of government – Nader would carry forward into his upcoming work on a wide variety of other issues.

Published in November 1965, *Unsafe at Any Speed* was dedicated to Frederick Hughes Condon, a friend of Nader's. Condon had been paralyzed in a 1961 car accident, when he was thrown halfway out of his car before being crushed.

Nearly 50,000 people were dying on American highways every year, *Unsafe* pointed out. A million more were injured. The cost to the country was great – due to the awful toll on many of its citizens and families, and all of the medical costs and property damage involved.

"Why?" Nader asked. Many readers of his book soon asked the same question.

The auto-safety hearings in Des Moines, Iowa, and Washington, D.C., followed the book's publication by a few months. General Motors' ill-conceived investigation of Nader then put the issue in newspaper articles across the land. President Lyndon Johnson and key members of Congress had the momentum they needed to get something done.

President Johnson signed the National Highway Traffic and Motor Vehicle Safety Acts on Sept. 9, 1966, after Congress passed the bills without a single "no" vote in either the U.S. Senate or House of Representatives. Nader, on hand to watch the signing, shook the president's hand afterward.

David Halberstam, who mentioned Nader in *The Best and the Brightest,* his famous book about the Vietnam War, calls *Unsafe at Any Speed* an enormously important book. Halberstam wrote that Nader's work "put the full moral pressure on the auto industry to bring about safety and consumer reforms."

"*Unsafe* is a great citizen text. It's not just about the auto industry, it's about the citizen revolution," Halberstam says. "I connect it with Rachel Carson's *Silent Spring*. Both are books demanding that if the government doesn't do anything, the citizens will act to create pressure and force the government to act.

"The two books say that if corporate interests are abusive and the government is silent, then citizens must act. And to arouse the public solely on the basis of a book is hard to do in a society as high powered as ours."

With President Johnson's signature less than a year after *Unsafe* was published, the auto industry now had safety standards to meet – thanks in large part to Nader's determination and hard work. With his wide acclaim and well-known name, Nader's next moves would involve applying his auto-safety experience to other industries and parts of society.

Chapter Ten

Nader's Raiders

An explosive mix of anger and enthusiasm engulfed America's college campuses in the late 1960s. Many students hated the Vietnam War. They demonstrated against what they saw as a pointless conflict, which was killing thousands of people their own age – both Vietnamese and American.

At times, the demonstrations turned violent. In May 1970, four students died at Kent State University in northern Ohio. National guard troops overreacted and fired into a crowd of students demonstrating on the campus. Images of innocent dead students shocked the country.

Assassinations, along with ongoing civil rights and environmental problems, also concerned the students. Civil rights leader and Nobel Peace Prize winner Martin Luther King, Jr. was shot to death in 1968. Nader friend and fan Sen. Robert Kennedy, who was running for president, also was murdered that year. America was in turmoil, and many young people were downright mad.

Nader attacked problems other than the Vietnam War. But he saw this mass of energy in student bodies across the nation as he traveled to campuses to deliver speeches. He decided to try and tap that energy.

Nader had an intense desire to change society in many ways – to create a better and safer quality of life for citizens everywhere. Many young people were drawn to his "gift of outrage," as he called it.

From the multitude of young believers inspired during his round of 1968 college visits, Nader chose seven to join him and work on the problems of corporate greed and government ineffectiveness. Soon after, these seven were dubbed "Nader's Raiders" in a story in *The Washington Post* – though their work hardly had the feel of a sudden attack or assault. Much of it entailed looking over documents page by page and compiling research. Yet the impacts of their work were great.

The Raiders first took on the U.S. Federal Trade Commission (FTC). The FTC's mission involved protecting consumers from advertising tricks, inferior products and other unfair business practices. But the commission had become an ineffective and poorly run government agency. Many of its top officials had landed their jobs through political favors rather than their knowledge and skills.

The Raiders searched FTC files and spoke with employees. The report they released in 1969 painted a picture of wrongdoing and clumsy performance. It brought respect and admiration to the Raiders and their work for Nader. It also brought needed change to the FTC.

President Richard Nixon, who took office in January 1969, ordered a government study of the commission. That study confirmed the findings of the Raiders' report. Nixon then named a new head of the agency, who undertook a major reorganizing effort.

The agency quickly turned into the consumer-advocate group it was meant to be. The FTC issued numerous warnings and complaints in the following years. In one case, for example, the commission revealed a contest by McDonald's restaurants that awarded only $13,000 of its advertised $500,000 in prize money.

The Raiders continued their investigations under Nader's

leadership. They focused on the problems created when corporations and special-interest groups influenced government agencies – agencies that were supposed to protect citizens.

They also produced a series of popular books on numerous topics. Some of the books covered their "raids" on various government agencies, while others looked into issues such as food safety, nursing homes, and water and air pollution. More than a dozen books involving the Raiders were published by 1972.

Nader's and the Raiders' efforts in those years spurred several significant consumer-related laws, including the Coal Mine Health and Safety Act and the Occupational Safety and Health Act, both of which still help save lives today. They also brought about important changes in meat and poultry inspection laws.

As well, Nader's auto-safety legacy continued. The U.S. government approved an ongoing stream of auto-safety regulations, making cars and highways safer for American citizens.

The Raiders worked tirelessly for Nader even though he wasn't always the easiest boss to please. He placed high demands on their time and talent and couldn't pay them much money. Although he set an example for them by working nonstop day and night, some Raiders came to believe he expected too much work and dedication. His high expectations and pushing of people who worked for him would cause him trouble in the years ahead.

I n 1969, Nader took a big step. He created an organization to support both his and the Raiders' ongoing efforts. Calling it the Center for the Study of Responsive Law, Nader set up a nonprofit effort designed to support consumers. He funded it through grants and private donations.

Scientists, lawyers, engineers and others worked together at

Ralph Nader often visited his hometown of Winsted, Conn., after moving to Washington, D.C. Here, Nader pulls a toboggan up Soldiers Monument Hill near his family's home in the late 1960s. He is followed by neighborhood children Joe, Mark, Kathy and Ann O'Brien. At the top of the hill, Ann gives the loaded toboggan a shove. In the bottom photo, Nader looks over the pile of laughing children.

the Center to conduct research and develop plans. Their goal was to protect consumers through either new laws or FTC-like reports that forced changes in the government. The Center still operates today, and Nader keeps his main office at its headquarters in Washington, D.C.

A large sum of money came Nader's way the following year. He had sued General Motors for harassment and invasion of privacy shortly after the investigation and related hearings ended four years earlier. After legal fees, the settlement he reached with the company in 1970 totaled about $280,000.

With money now available to support more work, Nader struck on another idea for an organization. "How about a law office that worked for the public's interest – not that of corporations or just individuals?" he wondered.

He called it the Public Interest Research Group (PIRG). It started out with 12 lawyers and a medical doctor. Each brought expertise in a different field to the effort. The PIRG staff worked on various subjects, such as banking, tax reform and health research.

"It was like a law office, but for public interest," Nader says. "We broke open a lot of new areas for several years. For instance, we were the first to bring action to create nonsmoking sections on public transportation. We presented the idea that nonsmokers had prior rights to those of smokers, which was unheard of back then.

"When I was a student at Princeton, lots of people smoked right in class," he says. "Classrooms were filled with smoke. Cigarette butts littered the floor. Can you imagine?"

In December 1969, Nader petitioned the Federal Aviation Agency to ban smoking on all airline flights. It took only a few years before Nader's idea received limited approval. Today, smoking is banned on all U.S. flights, as well as in many public areas. Second-hand smoke has become a well-known concern.

Two of the original PIRG members, Donald Ross and Jim Welch, were hired to focus on organizing students on college campuses across the nation. With Nader's help, they created a student-led movement that still exists today.

Nader hoped to spread the idea that young people could make a difference in government and corporate America. In the early 1970s, he spent more than a hundred nights of each year giving speeches at colleges and universities. His appearances usually attracted huge and excited crowds, which sometimes led to the formation of informal groups of student activists. However, although these students had plenty of enthusiasm, they often lacked resources like staff and funding.

A Nader appearance at the University of Oregon in the fall of 1970 launched the idea and provided a successful example for other campuses to follow. Soon, all seven schools in the state college system approved the establishment of the Oregon Student Public Interest Research Group, known as OSPIRG.

The student PIRG idea next took hold in Minnesota. There, a graduate student almost single-handedly organized a statewide movement of university and college students. More than 50,000 of the state's 90,000 students voted to start the Minnesota PIRG.

Each student PIRG was financed and run by students, but guided by a small professional staff of attorneys, scientists, organizers and others. To fund this staff, first a petition drive asked the ruling board at a college or university to establish a way to raise money.

Next, students voted whether or not to pay a small fee to set up a campus-wide PIRG. These annual dues of two to five dollars automatically were added to the tuition of all students on campus, although people could opt to not pay the fee if they chose.

"The students created their own independent organizations, that was the important thing," Nader says. "They were not controlled by me or the Center, although they were obviously involved in the same movement."

To help spread the PIRG idea, Ross and Nader wrote a book called *Action for a Change*. It laid out all the steps needed to start more of the organizations. Soon students around the country were reading this how-to book and making plans of their own.

Chapter Eleven

The Student PIRGs

Ralph Nader first met Tom Ryan in 1971. He knew right away that Ryan wasn't like most students interested in public-interest work. First, Ryan was a college student majoring in business administration – a course of study not pursued by many students who wanted to join Nader's citizen movement.

Maybe Ryan was confused, Nader thought. Didn't he realize the PIRG movement Nader was helping create on college campuses often involved taking on big business?

Secondly, Ryan wanted to become a vice president at Ford Motor Company. Why then, Nader wondered, was this 20-year-old student interested in the automobile industry's number one enemy – someone who had humiliated U.S. car manufacturers by revealing their abysmal safety record?

Ryan helped Nader with his bags at the St. Louis airport. On the half-hour drive to St. Louis University, the young man explained his interest in Nader's work and why he was picking Nader up. Ryan was president of the university's student activities board, which brought speakers like Nader to the campus. Maybe the college junior wasn't so confused after all, Nader decided.

"It was strange. I wanted to work for Ford, but at the same time I also related to students in liberal arts who were leading the anti-war and environmental movements on campus," Ryan says. "Nonetheless, I wanted to work from within corporate America.

"I had always been very practical, and I figured I could accomplish a lot more as an executive of a company – where the power base really is – than by simply protesting outside the system. I agreed with Ralph's criticism of the auto industry. But I believed I could maintain my idealistic spirit about change and still work within corporate America."

During the ride from the airport, Ryan told Nader why he wanted to work in marketing for Ford Motor Company. By working for a large corporation, he reasoned, he could have a greater impact in making it more progressive, rather than by working from the outside.

"Ralph and I had a great conversation during the drive to campus," Ryan says. "But before we got there, he had turned the tables on me. He told me what other students in Minnesota and Oregon were doing to start student-funded organizations that would allow them to have an impact on society right away."

Nader told Ryan that he had missed his time in the auto industry by about 50 years. Ford needed Ryan five decades earlier during the age of production, he said, but in the 1970s, America itself needed Ryan more than Ford did. The country needed people with the drive, brains and values to move into careers where they could have a positive impact on society as a whole. When Ryan said again that he was a marketing and business administration student, Nader told him that the PIRG movement needed more business-people to contribute their talents and expand the movement.

"He challenged me on the spot, during the ride from the airport," Ryan says. "'Why wait for 20 or 30 years to reach a position of power in the auto industry,' he asked me, 'when you can have

Ralph Nader makes a point on a television show in the mid-1970s, one of many television appearances he made during the decade.

a position of power in society today by creating a PIRG at St. Louis University?'"

The themes of Nader's speech that night stirred Ryan. However, when he decided to start a PIRG at St. Louis University the next day, Nader was gone – off to his next stop. He hadn't left a phone number.

Through Nader's speakers bureau, Ryan learned that his next speech was at Brigham Young University in Provo, Utah. He called various campus offices trying to leave a message for Nader to call him. He had no luck. Finally, he called the auditorium where Nader's speech would take place that night. A maintenance worker setting up chairs answered the phone.

"I have a message for Ralph Nader," Ryan said. "Will you be at the speech tonight?" When the worker replied yes, Ryan asked him to pass along the information.

Nader called late that night. "From the way your message was delivered," he said, "I thought it must be important."

Ryan said he wanted to start a PIRG in St. Louis. Nader gave him phone numbers for organizers in Washington, D.C., who helped him get started. Not long afterward, students at St. Louis University and nearby Washington University voted to assess themselves a four-dollar fee to support MOPIRG – the Missouri Public Interest Research Group.

Today, Ryan still vividly remembers that first meeting with Nader.

"I was immediately struck by his intensity," Ryan says. "He had a message and was passionate about it – to the point that it was overpowering. His logic and intense commitment to democracy also impressed me.

"I thought I was picking up some consumer advocate at the airport. Instead, within 30 minutes, I realized I was picking up the reincarnation of Thomas Jefferson. Ralph had captured the essence of what we know as Jeffersonian democracy – a society where everyone participates. He had a tremendous passion for this, and that is what hooked me."

Ryan ended up spending 13 years working for the PIRG he helped create in Missouri. He became its first student president. After receiving an undergraduate degree in business, he remained on the PIRG's board of directors while he attended law school at St. Louis University. With law degree in hand, Ryan then became MOPIRG's executive director in 1977 and worked in that capacity until he left the organization in 1984.

"And here it is, now almost 30 years since I first met Ralph, and the PIRG movement is still happening," Ryan says. "This one idea Ralph had and worked to make a reality is still having an impact in local communities across the country – much more impact than just one person ever could have. The PIRG movement is bigger than Ralph – and that's the way he wanted it."

The PIRGs set themselves apart from many other movements by actually participating in government processes, not by simply protesting against them. The PIRGs became players in the system, and quickly discovered they could affect the outcome of government decisions.

"We realized that it took lawyers and scientists to take part in many hearings," Ryan says. "You can't just participate by protesting. You also need to be a part of the process in order to influence various government decisions."

For example, in New Hampshire in the early 1970s, the state's PIRG helped lead a battle against a planned $600 million oil refinery project. The project was supported by the state's governor and largest newspaper, among others.

Backers of the refinery funded a huge public relations campaign to sway residents in the towns of Durham and Rye. Residents of those towns previously had voiced their disapproval of the project and prompted "no" votes by their town councils.

Refinery supporters turned to the state legislature when the campaign failed. The supporters figured economic concerns would rule out over any small-town environmental worries. Refinery supporters worked on a bill to overthrow the state's home-rule tradition. Home rule allows citizens the right to decide what takes place in their communities in certain situations.

Again, supporters of the project failed, due mainly to the actions and organizing efforts of the state's PIRG. Siding with their constituents – supposedly "powerless" citizens – New Hampshire legislators refused to pass the bill. The refinery project failed.

In Massachusetts, MASSPIRG placed an initiative on the state's ballot in 1986 aimed at reducing the use of toxic chemicals. Voters approved the measure by the largest margin of any initiative in the state's history. Similar efforts by PIRGs in Oregon and Washington the following year convinced state legislators and chemical industry officials to sit down and negotiate toxic-use reduction laws in those states. Today, a national set of laws and system of regulations are in place to deal with this issue.

Other PIRGs tackled issues such as recycling, pollution, energy, and public health and safety. The groups also provided training for thousands of students. This training continues today, producing wave after wave of students working to solve numerous problems in today's society.

"The PIRGs have helped teach people the real-world meaning of citizenship – given them a taste of citizen action," Nader says.

"They have shown them what can be done and given them tools they can use throughout their lives."

Today there are PIRGs in 24 states, and 17 more operate in Canada. Each is independent in its operation, yet all share similar agendas and goals. A national organization called U.S. PIRG formed in 1983. It serves as a national, Washington-based lobbying office working for the state groups.

Through the PIRGs, Nader created organizations of political action and societal change that could easily be used by students – or anyone else. He calls the PIRGs laboratories of democracy – places where people can experiment with their ideas and try to change the systems of government.

"And he wasn't trying to acquire power for himself. He was trying to disperse power, which is the basis of democracy," Ryan says. "He wanted to place power into the hands of a lot of citizens, who would then collectively deal with government in their search for a better society.

"Ralph understood that you had to actually take part in the operations of government institutions, not just write letters or hold protests. And without fanfare, the PIRGs he helped start are still having an impact, as are a lot the people he brought into the movement."

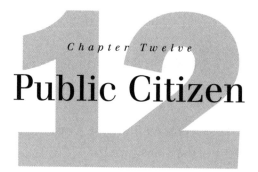

Chapter Twelve

Public Citizen

With several effective organizations in place, Ralph Nader could have slowed down, watched them grow and simply monitored their progress. Other people could now pick up the bulk of the workload. But Nader knew something was missing, and his energy level and enthusiasm still ran high.

He asked a close friend and associate what she thought a good next step might be. Joan Claybrook had an instant answer.

"I told him he should form a lobbying group – work to present ideas to members of Congress and persuade them to vote in favor of our public-interest work," she says. "It was a different idea from the research and law-based efforts he had started before, yet very important."

From that spark of an idea would rise an important group named Public Citizen. The organization, which is still at work today with the support of more than 150,000 members, is based in Washington, D.C. It focuses on issues of public interest, such as health, safety and political reform.

A Georgia congressman for whom Claybrook worked in 1966 wanted to meet Nader and talk about auto safety. But when Claybrook first tried to find Nader, it took her forever.

"First, I couldn't find his phone number anywhere," she says, laughing as she remembers her search for the very private Nader. "I had to track it down from someone at *The Washington Post.* Then I called and called. He was never there. Finally, I called him at midnight. He answered, a little upset with whoever was calling him that late at night."

That phone call began an impressive working relationship and friendship that has now bridged four decades. Claybrook runs Public Citizen today and as its president, talks and works with Nader constantly.

In 1966, the two started working together on the issue of auto safety. After Nader met with her boss, Rep. James Mackay, Claybrook began working on the first-ever, auto-safety regulatory bill. Her work on drafting the legislation would end up as part of the historic auto-safety bill that President Johnson signed in September 1966.

Claybrook then went to work at the National Highway Traffic Safety Administration, which had been created thanks to Johnson's signature. But in 1970, she decided to take a huge pay cut and come to work for Nader. She became one of the original PIRG members and also attended law school at night.

Not long after Claybrook came on board, Nader took on a massive project involving the U.S. Congress. He asked Claybrook to head up the yearlong effort. Called the Congress Project, the idea involved investigating the record of every single member of the U.S. Senate and House of Representatives. Nader hoped the effort would help the public decide who to vote for, as well as keep members of Congress honest and working for the people.

Claybrook and her small staff lined up volunteers in every state to complete some of the work. They also conducted interviews with all the members. In the end, they wrote 30-page profiles on each member of Congress and published them in a book.

The book made a splash at first, rising up the bestseller list. But it didn't have the impact Nader had hoped for, and it cost a lot of money to produce. He moved on to other projects, although he would later revisit the Congress Project idea.

At the same time, Nader's flagship organization Public Citizen was taking off, riding a wave of support provided by thousands of American citizens. Two mailings in 1971 to gather support worked extremely well. They attracted more than 60,000 members who donated more than a million dollars to the effort.

Nader created Public Citizen as an umbrella-type organization. Under that "umbrella," a number of different groups would tackle various problems and issues. For instance, two of the first efforts were the Health Research Group, headed up by Dr. Sidney Wolfe, and the Litigation Group, run by Alan Morrison.

Under the Public Citizen banner, these two groups could focus on their work to improve the country's healthcare and court systems. Public Citizen, on the other hand, took care of ongoing fundraising and bookkeeping work – the everyday business of running a nonprofit organization. Nader understood that funding was crucial in order to be successful in his work.

By forming another Public Citizen group in 1973, Nader returned to the idea of monitoring Congress. Claybrook helped start and lead the effort, called Congress Watch. Its goal was to work with Congress to pass laws that helped consumers and controlled corporations.

Claybrook remembers well the early days of Public Citizen and its various groups, especially the need to keep costs down. Nader was a tough boss when it came to spending money donated by the public.

Joan Claybrook speaks at one of many press conferences she has attended as president of Public Citizen.

"We couldn't make long-distance phone calls from the office," she says. "We had to go out and use pay phones, so we'd be aware of how long we were on the phone. And at first we didn't have a copy machine."

However, that situation soon changed at Public Citizen's main office. Photocopy machines were considered luxuries back then.

Unlike today, not every office had one. Nonetheless, the Litigation Group's Morrison said he wouldn't take the job if he didn't have a copier. He knew how useful they were from his previous legal work. Nader relented and purchased one.

Claybrook, who ran Congress Watch from a separate office closer to the U.S. Capitol Building, also made a request for a copy machine. But Nader drew the line on one copier. This setback, however, ended up pointing Claybrook in a new and successful direction.

"Because we had no copier, I told my staff to limit the fact sheets we gave to Congress to one page," she says. "My staff didn't like it at first, but the members of Congress loved it. They were so busy that they welcomed just one page of reading. It became a trend."

One of Public Citizen's greatest achievements involves freedom of information. When Congress passed the Freedom of Information Act (FOIA) in 1966, it gave the public access to lots of information held by the federal government. Except in a few sensitive areas, such as national security, the FOIA grants anyone the right to request and receive any document or file from any part of the federal government.

The act also allows citizens to sue the government in federal court, if necessary, to force its agencies to release information. It provides an effective way to hold government and business responsible for their actions.

Within a few years of the passage of the FOIA, however, corporations and government agencies had learned how to stall and limit the amount of information they had to reveal to the public. Nader, always a strong supporter of open government, became frustrated with the lack of power the act now carried and worked to change it.

First, he started the Freedom of Information Clearinghouse to help people use the act to gather information. Over the years, the Clearinghouse has sued the government several hundred times to force the release of vital information. Secondly, Nader worked to improve the existing FOIA and make it stronger.

"Secrecy ruins democracy," Nader says. "Information, on the other hand, helps support it. If you don't know and can't find out, you can't do anything. But the more you know about your government, such as what it's doing with your tax dollars, the more you can take part in it – by opposing it, improving it or supporting it."

Finally, in 1974, the FOIA was strengthened when new measures were added to the existing law. For instance, federal agencies could no longer stall. They had to respond to requests within two weeks.

Also, people or groups who successfully sued government agencies to obtain information could recover their attorneys' fees from the government. This, of course, made government agencies less likely to challenge the release of information.

"The changes in 1974 really made the Freedom of Information Act work," Nader says. "It gave it a lot more teeth and ability to do good."

And the FOIA has done plenty of good. Journalists and citizen organizations around the country have learned to use the tool to investigate thousands of cases of government mistakes and wrongdoing. They've uncovered dangerous products, environmental problems, and lots of cases of government waste and misconduct.

For instance, Public Citizen relied on the FOIA to reveal that a drug company and the government were hiding information about bad drug reactions that some people experienced. In fact, one drug played a role in the deaths of 50 elderly patients. Some employees at the drug company were charged with crimes and prosecuted.

Investigations and revelations such as these have allowed millions of Americans to better understand how their government works. And if they choose, citizens can now take part in influencing various government decisions.

Public Citizen turned to the Freedom of Information Act for another big battle in the 1970s. It used the act to gather information about all of the safety problems and malfunctions that occurred at nuclear power plants around the country. That information would in turn play a role in a huge citizen uprising – the battle over nuclear power.

Chapter Thirteen

Nuclear Power

The car inched forward through the crowd. People held up banners. Others waved signs in front of the car. "Home of Nuclear Power," many of them read.

Ralph Nader, a passenger in the car, had come to hostile territory to argue against nuclear power. People were demonstrating against his appearance.

After flying to Spokane, Washington, Nader traveled south to the federal government's Hanford Site. Also known as the Hanford Nuclear Reservation, the site served as a plutonium production facility to produce nuclear weapons. The facility also conducted research on nuclear power.

Later, inside the auditorium at Hanford, a huge crowd buzzed with excitement and anticipation. Plenty of scientists, engineers and others in favor of nuclear power were on hand. They were there to root for their man, an atomic energy scientist. He soon would debate Nader on a public television show that would be broadcast across the country.

Nader made his points and held his own against the scientist during the Hanford debate. This alone was an accomplishment because the crowd was definitely against him.

"What other form of energy presents a national security risk and requires complicated evacuation plans?" he asked at one point. "What other form of energy presents a risk to future generations for the next thousand years? Is this what we need to boil water?"

The crowd roared its disapproval. So later in the debate, Nader tried a different approach.

"What if the ancient Babylonians had used a form of energy that left us with thousands of years of deadly wastes? What would we think of them?" he asked. "You people would be well advised to hit the books again and start studying something else, because it's all over for nuclear power. Some day, you'll realize the problems involved with it."

The Hanford crowd, of course, didn't like these statements any better.

(Today, the Hanford Site is involved in one of the world's largest and most expensive environmental cleanup projects. For several decades, operations at Hanford released radioactive materials into the environment, which now must be cleaned up.)

Nader first became interested in nuclear power in the early 1970s, when he heard of frightening research about this new and expanding form of energy. One study, included in a government report, said a major accident at a nuclear power plant could affect an area the size of Pennsylvania. Learning this, Nader asked members of Congress to look into the safety of nuclear power. His request led to the first national hearings on this controversial and complex method of producing electricity.

About this time, the government estimated that 1,000 nuclear plants would be operating in the United States by the year 2000. It said that about 100 of those plants would be in California. If those plants were equally spread up and down the state's coast, that would mean one nuclear plant every ten miles.

Leaders of the nuclear power industry weren't concerned about Nader. They had momentum on their side. More than 20 nuclear plants already were built, and many more were planned. They knew they couldn't be stopped. One industry leader even told *The New York Times* that, "Nader is too late on this one. He can't stop us."

"Of course, that's all I had to hear," Nader says today.

Nader's concerns rose above just the safety factors involved in operating nuclear plants, which the government was now looking into. He also asked questions about the disposal of the radioactive waste produced at the plants. Where would the waste be sent? How would it be stored? Too many times, the answers were not very clear, he says, as if the industry planned to worry about those problems later on.

Ever mindful of consumers, Nader also brought up the high costs involved with nuclear-power technology. U.S. nuclear plants had been both expensive to build and expensive to run. As well, permanently closing them down could cost as much as building them because of the deadly radioactive wastes involved.

Tax money even had been used in large amounts to support nuclear power research and operations. Everyone uses electricity, Nader argued, so why should they have to pay more for it than is necessary – and face possible safety risks, as well?

Gradually, the public became aware of the many problems involved with nuclear power. Small groups of concerned citizens began organizing in places where plants were being built or planned.

In 1974, Nader and Joan Claybrook decided to give these small groups a national presence to rely on for help. They formed another Public Citizen effort – this one called the Critical Mass Energy Project. Critical mass is a term involving nuclear reac-

Nader's Achievements Noted in Many Publications

Over the years, hundreds of magazines and newspapers have written about Ralph Nader and his many different efforts. Several publications have included him on impressive lists they have created to honor important people.

For instance, in October 1999, the *Los Angeles Times* included Nader on its list of "The 50: People Who Most Influenced Business This Century." Nader was listed at No. 29 and noted as "the father of the modern consumer movement."

In 1990, *Life* magazine published a special issue titled, "The 100 Most Important Americans of the Century." Appropriately, Nader was featured on the same page as Rachel Carson, the author of *Silent Spring* who warned the world about the dangers of chemicals such as DDT. The magazine called Nader the "symbol of the citizen's right to know."

In the photo of Nader published in the issue, he is a young man. He is seated at an open table, speaking into a microphone at a government hearing. He is wearing big Army-like boots, laced up to the top, revealing the independent character he is.

"He was the champion we never knew we needed against an enemy we never suspected was there," stated *Life's* article about Nader. "When Nader was done [taking on the auto industry], we had become a nation of suspicious 'consumers' who realized that what was good for General Motors might be calamitous for the rest of us."

In 1974, the magazine
U.S. News and World Report *ranked*
Ralph Nader *as the fourth most influential person in the United States.*

In 1974, a national survey by the magazine *U.S. News and World Report* listed Nader as the fourth most influential person in the United States. Nader was pictured on the cover of the issue, along with other important American figures, under the headline, "Who Runs America?" President Richard Nixon topped the poll, followed by Secretary of State Henry Kissinger.

"Mr. Nader came through in survey comments characterized as 'a man you can trust,'" the magazine stated.

tions, but Nader saw the term as the "critical mass" of public support needed to stop nuclear power.

That year, Public Citizen held a huge Critical Mass conference. It attracted more than a thousand "anti-nuclear" activists. A follow-up conference, which drew as many people, was held the following year.

"The conferences served as training sessions," Nader says. "We linked people with experts in the nuclear field and lots of other sources of information. Leaders emerged from these long and intense weekends, along with lots of well-informed people ready to take on nuclear power."

The conferences showed the people attending, who were mostly members of small anti-nuclear groups, that they were part of a larger movement – that they weren't alone. Public Citizen also supported these groups with financial donations as they struggled to grow and become more effective.

In addition, the Critical Mass Energy Project conducted research and produced reports about the nuclear power industry. These reports detailed the many problems with nuclear power. They also presented information about other forms of energy less likely to hurt the environment or consumers' pocketbooks.

Several anti-nuclear rallies on the East Coast attracted thousands more people to the issue. Nearly 400,000 people gathered to protest against nuclear power at rallies in New York City and Washington, D.C. Huge events such as these also attracted lots of media attention and forced the nation to take a hard look at the issue.

While some support for nuclear power continued at the end of the 1970s, a bad accident at the Three Mile Island plant in Pennsylvania essentially ended the debate. The industry's stance on the safety of nuclear power was shattered. No new plants were ordered after the near-tragic 1979 accident, and other plans for new plants were cancelled. Nader, Claybrook and Public Citizen had played a major role in stopping the spread of nuclear power.

(Seven years after Three Mile Island, the world's worst nuclear-power accident occurred at the Chernobyl plant in the Soviet Union. The accident resulted in an explosion and fire, which spread radioactive material over thousands of miles. The disaster killed thousands of people and affected millions more. In the late 1990s, another less-severe accident occurred in Japan. There a worker mistakenly caused an explosion involving nuclear materials. Today, there are just over 100 nuclear power plants in the United States, and no more are being built or planned.)

O ver nearly 30 years since its founding, Public Citizen has undertaken all kinds of efforts to help strengthen America's democracy. It has worked to protect workers from dangerous chemicals and other hazards. It has forced corporations to be responsible for dangerous and defective products, as well as their impacts on the environment. And it has worked to make government agencies accountable to American citizens – the people they were created to serve.

Nader founded Public Citizen as a way to support the consumer movement he helped create. His idea involved using citizen action and community involvement to put pressure on government and corporations – and create a better form of democracy.

"People were getting hurt by unsafe drugs, cars and other dangerous products," Nader says. "And they were being harmed by corporate crime and pollution, and by government secrecy and misconduct. So we decided to work on those problems because government and corporations should be accountable to the people who use their products and services."

When Nader founded Public Citizen, he chose a quote by President Thomas Jefferson to represent the group's overall effort. "Patriotism is not a short and frenzied burst of emotion, but the long and steady dedication of a lifetime," Jefferson said.

The battle to control the excesses of corporations and the government never ends. Indeed, generation after generation must keep watch and continue the battle.

Although Public Citizen has had many successes over the past three decades, the organization realizes that it must have many more in the future. Victories on many fronts are needed in order to protect the rights of average Americans.

Chapter Fourteen

Discontent

The letter started out nicely enough. "Dear Joan," Nader wrote. But by the time his letter to Joan Claybrook ended, so did their lengthy friendship and successful working relationship.

For awhile, anyway.

Nader's letter, which was released to the media, called for her resignation. It said she had turned against consumers by giving auto companies six more years before they had to install air bags in cars.

Claybrook left Public Citizen in 1977 to run the National Highway Traffic Safety Administration. She and many other consumer activists were invited to work for President Jimmy Carter in his new administration after the 1976 election. After just eight months on the job, however, Claybrook came under fire.

"It was a terribly critical letter," Claybrook says. "I didn't know what had caused Ralph to have this atomic explosion. Everyone was coming up to me and saying, 'What's going on?'"

When Claybrook first took the job, plenty of people were shocked that a former member of Nader's Raiders was running the highway administration. This was a position of power that could bring many more pro-safety changes to the auto industry. But Nader said six years was too long for air bags to become standard equipment.

From Nader's perspective, the auto industry had too much influence on the air-bag decision, and he took a firm stance on the other side of the issue. He said the letter was the most effective way he could make his point.

Nonetheless, he was heavily criticized for his attack on Claybrook, who was one of his strongest supporters. News stories about the air-bag disagreement portrayed Nader as the bad guy. Claybrook's mother, however, came to Nader's defense.

"My mother called and said, 'Look, Ralph doesn't understand that he has hurt you. He just thinks he's working on policy. You have to forgive him,'" Claybrook says. "I told her, 'Well, I'll take about a year before I do that.'"

It didn't take that long for Claybrook's anger to start to subside.

"Ralph and I should be able to criticize each other without undermining our friendship," she told a national magazine, *People Weekly,* not long after the incident. "It is hard to be totally outraged with someone when you know that your goals are the same."

Nader felt he had to fight for consumers, whether a friend was involved or not. He always worked to keep pressure on the government, and his attack on Claybrook and the air-bag delay was simply more of the same.

But if the public didn't like Nader's treatment of Claybrook, that was just the beginning. Many negative images haunted Nader during the late 1970s. His ability to gain support and create change became increasingly limited. In fact, winning battles for consumers would never be easy again.

For one thing, corporations had simply had enough. Nader had embarrassed them, gotten them to admit wrongdoing and forced them to treat consumers better. Large companies and their lobbyists fought back against the consumer movement. They used

Even in his 80s, Ralph Nader's father, Nathra Nader (center), kept up his activist ways. Here he leads a 1977 march in downtown Winsted, Conn., protesting congressional pay raises.

their money and power to once again influence government decision making.

Business lobbyists also painted Nader as a man who had gone

too far, asked for too much. They succeeded, at least in part, as consumer issues faded from the public's eye. Instead, inflation and other economic concerns became the main issues of the day.

Another negative factor involved the media. Nader, along with all of his various groups and activities, had been all over the news for about a decade. But now he was old news. People in the media stopped paying as much attention to him as they once had.

"If you are a media event – as Ralph was for quite awhile – eventually you will wither by the media. You're not new anymore. Getting your story out becomes difficult," Claybrook says. "Plus, Ralph is hard hitting. He tells it like it is. Because of that, some people thought he was too brash, too forceful."

Nader's habit of "telling it like it is" also got him in trouble with other people, especially members of Congress. Many of them supported a lot of Nader's ideas. But if they disagreed with him in the slightest, they faced Nader's anger.

Some members of Congress grew tired of what they perceived as his all-or-nothing attitude. But as Nader saw it, he was working to make America's democratic system work as well as it possibly could, no matter the consequences.

On top of all this, Nader remained intensely private. He felt it was no one's business where he lived or how he lived or how he spent money. Because of this, some people saw him as paranoid or overly secretive.

Also, Nader never married or had a family. He continued to work nonstop, seven days a week. He didn't own a car or television. For a popular American figure, which Nader had become, all of this was very unusual.

Portions of the public and media resented his desire for a private life outside of his very public work activities. Rumors circled about how poorly he treated some of his co-workers. A former

Raider and Nader friend even wrote a scathing book about him, calling Nader arrogant and authoritarian.

Because of all this, many people thought of Nader as a cold and unfeeling man, and a difficult boss as well. Some of these perceptions have haunted him ever since.

The late 1970s also dealt Nader one of his greatest defeats. He and Public Citizen had long worked for the creation of a federal agency to represent consumers in the day-to-day business of the federal government. Called the Consumer Protection Agency, it would have dealt with consumer interests in front of the government's various agencies.

Nader considered the agency an important and inexpensive idea that could do great good for the American public. It could monitor and intervene with government business on behalf of citizens. It would serve as a watchdog to ensure government agencies did their jobs and didn't cater to big business.

Corporations, however, fought hard against the consumer agency idea. They saw Nader's concept as a threat to their power. Because consumer issues weren't the priority they had been just a few years before, the idea narrowly failed to pass the U.S. House of Representatives in 1978.

"Sure, we've had some disappointments," Nader told *Time* magazine after the defeat. "But I didn't get into this business because I thought it was easy."

If the last years of the 1970s were tough on Nader, the 1980s were worse. He had to deal with a personal tragedy in his life, a drastic change in American politics and a potentially serious illness.

Chapter Fifteen

Tough Times

Nader began the decade of the 1980s by resigning as president of Public Citizen after nearly a decade as head of the organization. Joan Claybrook, fresh from her experience in government as head of the highway administration, took over Nader's leadership role at Public Citizen about a year later. The two had long since gotten over their quarrel of a few years before.

Nader wanted to turn his energies in many different directions, Public Citizen being just one of them. By now, Nader had helped create nearly 50 different organizations. Collectively, they worked on public-interest issues on many fronts, dealing with everything from the aviation industry to hazardous waste.

Nader faced a new challenge beginning in 1981 as well. That challenge involved President Ronald Reagan, whose new administration quickly changed course from that of President Jimmy Carter.

Much of Nader's work to date involved regulations that forced corporations and industries to follow laws or be held accountable by the government and the courts. Those regulations made businesses responsible for the pollution they created and the defective products they produced, as well as other unfair corporate practices.

But President Reagan and the people in his administration had different ideas. They wanted more power returned to corporations. All of these regulations were hampering business, they said. Fewer laws and less oversight were needed. Corporations across the country agreed with this thinking, and fully supported it with lobbying and donations of money.

Nader and many other people, of course, couldn't have disagreed more. Nader found himself defending the protections he had helped create for the American public.

"Suddenly, all we could do was play defense," Nader says. "And once you're on the defensive – trying to protect what already exists – it's hard to switch to offense. They were terrible times. We couldn't get our new ideas going."

The Reagan Administration set about reducing government regulations in many areas. For instance, the Environmental Protection Agency, which works to reduce pollution and other environmental dangers, had its budget drastically cut. This, in turn, severely limited the number of inspections and enforcement activities the agency could undertake to keep watch over various industries.

Nader noticed one trouble spot early on. But he couldn't raise awareness over it. The trouble spot involved the nation's "savings and loans" (S&Ls) banks. A lack of regulation, promoted by the Reagan Administration, had allowed the S&Ls to make risky investments with peoples' money. When those investments went bad, the collapse of the S&Ls threatened the nation's financial stability.

Congress eventually bailed out the S&L industry. The bailout cost American taxpayers about $500 billion. "That's a lot of wasted money that could have paid for a lot of healthcare. Perhaps a certain amount of regulation isn't such a bad idea," Nader kept saying, although few people were listening at the time.

"There are only a few ways to limit corporate greed. Government regulation and suing companies to hold them accountable are two of them," Nader says. "A lack of government regulation and oversight leaves consumers with no protection. I'm not anti-business, as some businesspeople seem to think. I'm just pro-people."

"Frustration" might seem a good word to describe Nader's mood in facing the losing battles of the 1980s. But he fought off a loss of hope and sense of futility. He remained determined to limit the damage and continue his fight for a fairer form of American democracy.

"There's a tendency for people – when they come up against a loss – to get derailed," Nader told *The Progressive* magazine in 1984. "What you've got to do is just get past it and, boom, come right back."

Unfortunately, Nader faced two more severe losses during the 1980s – that of his brother and his own health. Ralph's older brother Shafeek came down with prostate cancer and became very sick.

At the time, Nader was in the midst of a massive fight to protect people's rights to sue companies if they are injured. He visited 48 states in just four months. Then, during a debate at a college in April 1986, Nader noticed that his left eye wouldn't close.

"The next morning I woke up and the whole left side of my face was numb," he says. "I was traveling a lot, and this was the year that Shafeek was the sickest. It was a terrible time."

Nader had contracted Bell's Palsy, a mysterious disease that paralyzes nerves in the face. Many times, the disease will disappear in a few weeks. But Nader suffered with it for months.

"There's nothing you can do about it," Nader says. "My eyelid drooped over my eye, so I wore dark glasses to deal with it. It made for some interesting press conferences, and I even wore dark glasses on a television news show one time."

Ralph Nader worked hard throughout the 1980s, but the decade was a tough one for him. He lost his brother to cancer in 1986, and he contracted the disease Bell's Palsy.

Although the disease frustrated him at times, causing his eye to constantly dry out and paralyzing part of his face, Nader learned to laugh about it. "At least today you can't accuse me of talking out of both sides of my mouth," he would say during speeches.

Then in August 1986, while Nader still fought his Bell's Palsy, Shafeek died. The loss devastated Nader. He retreated to his hometown in Connecticut for a few months and grieved over his brother's death.

"Losing my brother was one of the hardest things I've ever faced," Nader says. "I still miss him a lot."

Eventually, however, Nader knew his life and work had to continue. Although the 1980s had brought lots of tough times, all of the organizations he helped create still plowed ahead with their work. And those groups still needed his help.

With the arrival of the 1990s, many Americans once again grew concerned about the power corporations wielded over their lives. The expensive savings-and-loan disaster forced them to take notice, as did looming environmental problems.

At the same time, Nader considered a new approach. He had never been interested in running for political office. But maybe getting into politics wasn't such a bad idea, he now thought.

"When so many avenues are blocked, and you can't negotiate your proposals with Congress or work them through the court system, then politics becomes a possibility," he says. "Thomas Jefferson said our representative government is supposed to 'counteract the excesses of the monied interests.' But when the government is controlled by corporations – our new form of 'monied interests' – you have to get into politics."

Following that line of thinking, Nader ran as a "none-of-the-above" protest candidate in the 1992 New Hampshire presidential primary. He received a lot of votes considering he spent little or no money on his campaign.

And he enjoyed this new way to reach out to people. During the campaign, he talked about his hopes for American democracy. He also spoke about his plans to strengthen citizen movements and limit corporate power.

Nader's 1992 effort in New Hampshire served as a warm-up for the political effort he would undertake for the 1996 presidential election. That year, a lot of Americans would have the chance to vote for Ralph Nader as president. And for the first time in quite a while, Nader's ideas and thoughts would reach a much wider audience.

Chapter Sixteen

Running for President

R alph Nader paces the waiting room of NBC's Washington studio, anticipating his arrival on stage and the fast-paced questions that will follow. He walks to a nearby mirror and adjusts his red-striped tie. He lightly brushes his graying temples.

It is a Sunday morning in March 1996, and the television network's "Meet the Press" news program is under way. Nader hears the voice of Tim Russert, the show's host and moderator, say, "Coming up next: consumer advocate Ralph Nader. He's running for president, and the White House is concerned. We'll find out why after this."

Nader heads for the door, his pin-striped suit hanging loosely from his six-foot, four-inch frame. A stagehand meets him at the door and leads him to the bright lights of the set. When the commercial break ends, Russert asks bluntly, "Why are you running for president?"

"Because we're part of a larger and long-term movement to build democracy in concrete ways, to strengthen the roles of the citizen, taxpayer and consumer," says Nader, who is the Green Party's candidate for president. "And to compete with the two parties – tweedle-dee, tweedle-dum, Republican, Democrat – which are increasingly of, by, and for big business. The dominance of corporations – over our government, over our marketplace, over labor, over small business – is getting completely out of hand and is on a collision course with democracy."

Nader sits hunched over a large wooden desk, across from Russert. Pages of notes are scattered before him and a coffee mug sits near his right hand. A bank of television screens creates a wall behind him, each lit up with the words "Meet the Press."

"So two parties can't serve this country well enough?" Russert asks.

"The two-party system that now exists in America provides far too narrow a choice, especially when the two parties cozy up in the laps of the major corporations more and more," Nader says. "We've got to have competition and a broader democratic agenda that enlists the energies of the American people."

N ader faced dozens of interviewers like Russert on national television and radio shows throughout 1996. He also gave more interviews for numerous magazine and newspaper articles. He wanted to expand a growing political movement in America – the creation of a viable third party to challenge America's long-standing Democratic and Republican parties.

This idea became legitimate in 1992 when Ross Perot and his Reform Party received nearly 20 percent of the vote. Perot's showing helped spell the end to George Bush's presidency, and President Bill Clinton won the election.

Through his 1996 campaign as the Green Party's candidate for president, Nader hoped to inspire people to be more involved, to play a bigger role in shaping the country. While he knew he stood no chance of becoming the next U.S. president, Nader still attracted a sizable following.

Nearly 700,000 people in 21 states voted for him, placing him fourth in the national tally behind Clinton, Bob Dole and Ross Perot. In Oregon, he received more than four percent of the vote. And in California, more than 230,000 people voted for Nader.

Nader had long realized the problems of America's two-party political system. As a youth, he told his father, Nathra, "Dad, we need a third political party."

"I'll settle for a second," his father answered, who was troubled even back then that the Democratic and Republican parties were essentially one and the same.

"When the wealth of the top one percent of the American people is equal to the 90 percent at the bottom – when there's so much wealth and power in so few hands – the country gets in trouble," Nader says today. "I think democracy is the best mechanism for solving problems ever devised, but our democracy here in America is in need of repair and restoration."

With the 1996 presidential campaign in full swing, Nader traveled to New Mexico and southwestern Colorado in October to give several speeches. Nader was the center of attention at an Albuquerque press conference, held after he spoke to students at the University of New Mexico. Surrounded by reporters, students and Green Party members, Nader patiently answered questions.

One woman desperately wanted to buy him lunch. After being asked about his lunch plans three or four times, Nader politely told her that box lunches were the only thing that would work. His next stop was Durango, Colorado – a four-hour drive to the north – and another speaking engagement at the town's Fort Lewis College that evening.

Ralph Nader speaks in his hometown of Winsted, Conn.

Nearby, Melanie Peacock, a mother of three teenagers and a student at Fort Lewis, waited for Nader. She had come to Albuquerque that morning to drive Nader to the Colorado school. She was nervous about driving America's auto-safety expert to his next appointment.

"Do you have any rules for driving that I should know about?" she asked Nader before they hopped into a four-door rental car.

"Just the speed limit," Nader said. "That's all that matters to me."

With that, Peacock, Nader, an assistant and another Green Party member climbed in and took off. They talked about school, baseball, cloud formations and the towns they passed through as they traveled north.

A lot of people expect Nader to be very serious and not particularly friendly. The outgoing Peacock fell into that category. But her expectations soon changed.

"He had been a hero of mine since I was a teenager," says the 40-year-old Peacock. "For some reason I thought he'd be kind of dark and humorless. But he was relaxed, good-natured and easygoing. The ride was great."

After a quick stop in Cuba, New Mexico, for phone calls and some juice, the group pushed on to Colorado. Although they hit town just 20 minutes before the event, Nader was not upset. He got right to work. He held a quick press conference so local reporters could meet their deadlines, then headed for the stage.

His talk lasted two hours in front of a packed ballroom at the college. More than 800 people, both students and townspeople, filled the hall to overflowing. All of the chairs were filled. Part of the crowd had to stand up in back.

Nader discussed the concentration of corporate and political power that threatens the future of America. Similar situations have caused trouble in the past, he said, but citizen action has always helped solve the problems of too much power in too few hands.

"We can take back our government if we organize," he said. "If we don't go through life on our knees, if we don't grow up corporate, if we stand tall, if we believe that we count, then together we can be decisive."

After a loud and enthusiastic ovation at the end of his speech, Nader answered more than an hour's worth of questions before finally ending the event. Nonetheless, more people approached him afterward with further questions.

Nader wrapped up his day with a meal at the local Denny's restaurant, joining a group of about a dozen people, including his driver for the day, Melanie Peacock. Despite yet another long day, Nader was relaxed and personable.

At one point in the meal, someone pulled out a camera to have a picture taken with Nader. Soon more cameras appeared and a round of photographs ensued. Peacock took most of the photos. After about the fifteenth flash, Nader held his hands up to his face. "Stop, stop," he said with a laugh. "You're turning me into a celebrity."

Well after midnight, with the check paid, the group filed out of the restaurant. After saying goodbye to the other guests, Nader turned to Peacock. He thanked her for her driving, her conversation and, jokingly, for her photography work.

He then walked the two blocks to his room for the night at Durango's historic Strater Hotel. With that, another day of unusual presidential campaigning drew to a close for Ralph Nader.

Chapter Seventeen

The Green Party

N ader knew he had no chance of being elected president during the 1996 campaign. But he hoped his campaign would help spur the growth of a third party that could grow powerful enough to influence future U.S. elections.

He chose the Green Party – a political group that began in England and New Zealand as an anti-nuclear force, and went on to become a powerful part of the German Parliament. The U.S. Green Party began organizing in 1984 and has since formed parties in more than 25 states, including California and New York. As part of an international movement, the Green Party also is active in many other states and in more than 50 countries.

The party is united by its "key values," which include nonviolence, social justice, environmentalism, respect for diversity, global responsibility and community-based economics and democracy.

Nader signed on as the Green Party's presidential candidate in 1996 after 50 California party members sent him a letter. They offered him the Green Party's slot on the state's ballot. Nader accepted, but made it clear he would run as their candidate on his terms. He raised no money and accepted no campaign contributions. He aired no television commercials.

Nader asked the Green Party to do all of the campaign's organizing and a lot of the campaigning. He contributed by giving speeches, circulating videos, posting position papers on the Internet and giving lots of interviews.

"I wanted to give the Green Party more energy in the hope that they could begin making a difference, signing up more people, becoming a more visible alternative to the two major U.S. parties," Nader says. "I wanted to help inspire a new generation of activists – people who wanted to change politics."

Nader has much in common with the Green Party. The two share a common passion for grass-roots organizing and consumer-focused politics.

The U.S. Green Party and its more than 80,000 members sought greater political influence. Nader helped move them in that direction in 1996 by demonstrating what an alternative candidate could do. Although he spent basically no money, Nader stated his case for a new form of democracy by giving hundreds of media interviews across the country.

"Year after year, Americans are losing control over their government, over the marketplace, over their workplace and over the future for their children," he said in one of those interviews. "Of course, we don't want big government. But we do want and deserve a responsive and efficient government – one that works for ordinary citizens and keeps corporate power in check."

Nader's campaign revolved around what he calls "The Concord Principles." These principles aim at fixing a political system in America that he believes has moved far from the democracy that President Thomas Jefferson spoke of 200 years ago.

The Concord Principles outline various "tools of democracy," as Nader calls them. They include ideas like a "none-of-the-above" option for elections, 12-year term limits for politicians, public financing of campaigns, easier voter registration and an advisory national referendum process.

Under his referendum plan, citizens would not just vote on individuals and politicians. They also would vote on various proposals and issues. A national referendum would prompt more people to vote, Nader believes, which would only help democracy.

"The Elvis stamp is the only national issue we've ever voted on. Think of that," Nader says. "The federal government said, 'We want to know what version of the Elvis stamp you want. But don't even think about voting on healthcare.' That's absurd."

A national referendum would provide people with a direct say in their government, Nader explains. Although the voting would not create new laws or policies, it would send a powerful message. Politicians would have a hard time arguing against proposals supported by people with their votes.

Concerning the "none-of-the-above" ballot option, Nader would like to see the U.S. Congress and state legislatures pass laws allowing for "no-confidence" votes. Candidates would then have to compete with each other, along with an alternative "none-of-the-above" candidate. If the "none-of-the-above" choice received the most votes, the election would be canceled. A new election would then be started with a new set of candidates.

This would provide a solution to the problem of voters simply staying home in order to cast "no-confidence" votes, Nader believes. It also would force candidates to distinguish themselves from one another in positive ways – or face the humiliation of losing to "none of the above."

Not surprisingly, much of Nader's attention during the 1996 campaign focused on corporate power – a subject that has drawn his focus for decades. Nader repeatedly attacked the influence that large U.S. corporations hold over government, workers and consumers.

Attorney Charlene LaVoie (left) talks with Ralph Nader at the Community Lawyer's office in Winsted, Conn.

Ralph Nader (center) visits with a small group of people during a visit to his home state of Connecticut.

"Corporations have steamrolled the two main political parties," Nader said during the campaign. "We have a government of the Exxons, by General Motors and for the DuPonts. We're moving into a period of our history when the forces that work against corporate power are falling behind. They are being overwhelmed.

"The question is this: Is our government doing what a majority of its citizens want done? If it isn't, then something is wrong and should be changed. And this is a question not being asked by the other candidates."

Tom Ryan, Nader's old friend and former director of the Missouri PIRG, does a good job of describing Nader's passion and his political intentions.

"In many respects, Ralph is the person who we all were in grade school – back when we first read about Thomas Jefferson and the ideals of this country," Ryan says. "But unlike a lot of people today, Ralph still believes in the ideal that this can be a country 'by, for, and of the people.' And he believes in it so much that he's outraged by the fact that we no longer have a democracy that is controlled by its citizens."

Chapter Eighteen

Corporate Power

An elderly grandmother buys a cup of coffee at a McDonald's drive-through window. She is riding in a car driven by her grandson, who stops the car so she can add some cream and sugar to her drink.

She spills the coffee in her lap and suffers third-degree burns over six percent of her body. She spends eight days in the hospital and must undergo skin grafts. It takes her two years to fully recover from the coffee accident. She ends up with scars over 16 percent of her body.

In the end, she sues McDonald's and wins. She is awarded $2.9 million by a New Mexico jury in 1994.

Ridiculous, many people said at the time. A clumsy lady spilled coffee on herself. That's not McDonald's fault.

That's certainly what McDonald's and other large companies wanted the American public to think. And to a great extent, that perception spread across the country. People were mad about the lady who sued McDonald's over coffee and won. Our court system is broken, they said, and this is proof.

But the rest of the story is where a good example of corporate power can be found.

At first, the woman simply asked McDonald's to cover her medical expenses. She had never sued anyone before and she didn't use a lawyer. She asked for $15,000 to $20,000. McDonald's, in turn, offered her $800. She decided to file suit in state court.

The trial revealed a lot about McDonald's and its operations. The company required that its coffee be served at a very hot 190 degrees, which can destroy skin in seconds and was much hotter than coffee served by many other restaurants. And the company had a long history of its customers being burned by its coffee.

In fact, over a 10-year period, McDonald's knew of more than 700 people who had been burned by its coffee, the trial revealed. Children even had been burned when employees accidentally knocked hot coffee on them. Yet the company did nothing in terms of lowering the extreme temperature of its coffee or adequately warning people about the danger.

At the trial, a safety consultant for McDonald's basically said that with billions of cups of coffee served every year, 700 burn cases didn't really matter. This upset members of the jury. They knew that behind each one of those 700 cases was someone who had suffered a very painful injury, like the woman sitting in front of them in the courtroom.

The jury decided on $2.7 million in punitive damages to get McDonald's attention, not to make some grandmother rich. McDonald's knew its coffee could severely burn its customers – and had burned hundreds of them – but did next to nothing. Interestingly, the jury chose $2.7 million because it equaled two days' worth of coffee sales for McDonald's – not much for a company of that size.

In the end, the judge, while agreeing that McDonald's was in the wrong, reduced the amount of money the company had to pay

With years of practice behind him, Ralph Nader is comfortable speaking behind a wall of microphones. During his campaign for president in 2000, he continually gave speeches and attended press conferences.

to $640,000. Still a lot of money, but nowhere near almost $3 million. Then the company confidentially settled the case with the woman out of court, possibly for a lesser amount.

Unfortunately, because of the media and corporations' ability to influence public opinion, this case was blown way out of proportion. "This is crazy – suing over spilled coffee," a lot of people hollered after reading incomplete stories about the case and listening to late-night comedians make jokes about it.

"In reality, most juries only return big verdicts against corporations when someone presents a compelling case of irresponsibility that led to serious injury," Nader says in his never-ending fight to control corporate power. "But that doesn't stop corporations from arguing against the idea of being held accountable at all, or in a very limited fashion. In fact, punitive damages are awarded in only about two percent of cases."

Corporations today are fighting against cases like the burned grandmother with an effort called "tort reform." Tort law involves lawsuits such as the McDonald's case in which potentially wrongful acts have occurred. Weakening America's tort system is a very dangerous idea, Nader says, because juries are one of the few ways to protect people's rights to health and safety.

"A lot of products are a lot safer today because of our tort system," he says. "Chain saws have safety guards, for instance, and kids' pajamas are now fire resistant. Defective cars are more likely to be recalled. If tort reform passes, citizens will lose their rights – their access to their own courts to seek justice from companies that injure them.

"What's wrong with letting judges and juries decide the facts of individual cases like the McDonald's coffee case? They're the only ones who see, hear and evaluate the evidence, and the higher courts decide whether they performed properly."

Since his first encounters with the auto industry, Nader has worked to control the power of corporations in American society. Although he has had some successes, many dangers remain.

Corporations are powerful because they are so big and make so much money. By using that money, corporations have become big-time players in both American and world politics. Eighty percent of the money contributed to U.S. federal elections now comes from corporate interests.

That means corporations can control elections. They then have more power in the government than ordinary citizens. And that's not the form of democracy the founders of this country had in mind.

"Corporations are like octopuses. You cut off one tentacle and another one grows back," says Joan Claybrook, president of Public Citizen. "So it's important for citizen action to stay alive, otherwise we surrender the battle to the corporations and let them run the show."

One of Nader's biggest successes is that through his work he has forced corporations to behave differently today than they did a few decades ago.

"Corporations are now much more likely to recognize a hopeless cause and work toward a compromise," Claybrook says. "And they have to be more open in how they operate – thanks to Ralph's work – so finding those hopeless causes and other problems is easier."

"We need to get to a point where corporate honesty and fair dealing are more commonplace," Nader says. "And we need a government that works harder to stop corporate abuses when it comes to health, safety and the environment. If we can accomplish these things, we'll have a much fairer form of democracy, one that adequately protects its citizens."

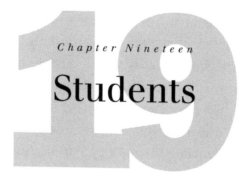

Chapter Nineteen

Students

No one in American public life has given more speeches on U.S. campuses than Ralph Nader over the past 30 years. The goal of all of those speeches? To inspire students to get involved and take on the sometimes difficult tasks of fighting corporate injustice and changing society.

When someone uses the common phrase, "You can't fight City Hall," Nader says, "Yes, you can. Here's how and here are some tools you can use. You can take on any public institution you want because, in essence, it is yours."

Today, that message remains inspirational for the thousands of students with whom Nader speaks during his travels. Many students believe the political process and government are overrun by money and corporate power. Nader helps them see that there is hope, that change for the better is still possible.

"I never talk down to students. There's no need. They can make great contributions to our civic life at early ages and may only need a small nudge to get going," he says. "American students are in the top two percent of people their age in the world in terms of health, education and ability to make a difference – thanks to the U.S. Constitution. Millions of people their age can only worry about where their next meal will come from."

Nader tries to connect college students' possibilities with successes of the past. Young people ended the Vietnam War, and they forced changes that protected the environment and provided civil rights for African-Americans. In his talks, Nader urges students to get involved.

"Right now, you are risk takers and have lots of opportunities. You are freer than most people," he says in his speeches to students. "You have your own newspapers, your own radio stations, your own laboratories and your own experts in the form of teachers. All you need is to have a higher estimate of your own worth in the life of our democratic society.

"You have about 15,000 days until you reach age 65, about 2,000 weeks until retirement," he tells them. "And didn't last week go by fast?"

When the laughter subsides, he continues.

"Who among you will be the leaders in saving the forests? Who among you will make our government work better? Who will solve the problems of our healthcare system? Many important movements have been started by students."

Although Nader has accomplished a lot and won many victories for common Americans during his lifetime, he has a hard time looking back at the past. All he can see, he says, is what still needs to be done in the future. And that is plenty.

Nader is so focused on the battles for citizens' rights that he has foregone having a family. A major sacrifice, to be sure.

"With the kind of work I do, I'm always short on time," Nader says. "Yet children deserve all the time their parents can devote to them. Plus, I can take on uncertainties because I don't have to worry about taking care of a family.

"I decided I couldn't do my work and have a family, too – not with the hours I put in," he continues. "I'm content with the knowledge that I'm working hard to protect all children."

Nader's sister, Laura, agrees with her brother's decision.

"If you're going to have a life like he has – where he works night and day – that's no life for a family," Laura says. "Unfortunately, people often associate that kind of dedication with negatives. But he's happy with his work, and he shows that one individual can do a lot."

Now in his 60s, Nader still works nonstop. He has long been known for his long workweeks. Today, they remain basically 80-hour, seven-day affairs. Many days he will work on a dozen different projects, providing his knowledge and support where needed. He also makes time to keep up with current affairs by reading four newspapers a day, as well as newsmagazines and other journals.

Nader's long-time friend and co-worker, Joan Claybrook, is still amazed and impressed with his efforts.

"He has helped people realize that they have a right to safety, a right to know and a right to participate," she says. "He still works on those basic rights every day. Everything he does is for the betterment of humanity. He believes people's health and safety should come first. And it's not a reach to say his work has saved tens of thousands of lives, if not millions.

"He is constantly helping people – with advice, contacts, media attention, whatever," she adds. "He has supported thousands of community efforts over the years, and helped teach and inspire lots of new leaders."

Along with continuing his efforts to support the more than 50 organizations he has created, Nader's work today continues to grow larger. For instance, he is fighting the resurgence of two ter-

*On Presidents' Day in February 2000, a few days before his 66th birthday,
Ralph Nader announced his bid for president and kicked off his 2000 campaign.*

rible diseases around the world – malaria and tuberculosis. Scientists once thought they had wiped out malaria, but about 40 percent of the world's population now face its threat. And tuberculosis has been reborn, managing to outdo most medicines developed by science to fight it.

"People ask me, 'What have you been doing?'" Nader says. "And I tell them, 'I'm doing more than ever. Look at our website.'" [www.essential.org]

Another of Nader's recent projects? His run at the U.S. presidency in 2000 with the Green Party, including the acceptance of donations from individual citizens to spread his message further, and being on the ballot in nearly every state, instead of less than half as he was in 1996.

"Not a single candidate who I am aware of ever looks at the

American people and says to them, 'Do you want to be more powerful against the rich and powerful?'" he said during the announcement of his 2000 run for president. "I do, and that's why this campaign is so different."

Nader pointed out that 20 percent of America's children grew up in poverty during the economic boom of the 1990s, far higher than any other comparable wealthy country in the world. The number of Americans without health insurance grows every year, as well.

The Green Party was given a boost by Nader's candidacy in the 1996 campaign. With Nader as its candidate, the party attracted more young people to its new form of progressive politics. Thus, Nader chose to take part in the party's 2000 campaign.

"Both the Green Party and I seek a broader discussion of the larger issue – how corporate power is concentrated and abused in our government to limit human potential and hurt innocent people," Nader says of his 2000 effort. "People need to begin taking back their government and restoring the true balance of power that the founders of this country envisioned more than 200 years ago."

Over the years, Ralph Nader has maintained a vision that focuses on helping citizens create a government that better meets the needs of its people. In doing so, he has had a huge impact on America by working to provide safety and well-being for its citizens. It's nearly impossible to go anywhere or do anything without coming across something touched by Nader's lifetime of accomplishments.

Nader's work remains important and relevant today, says longtime friend and fellow author David Halberstam.

"The abuses are as great as ever," he says. "Our society and economy are changing rapidly, and those changes provide even

Ralph Nader has been an avid and enthusiastic reader since he was a young boy. Today, he reads four newspapers and various newsmagazines every day, along with several books every month.

more opportunities for abuse. All kinds of threats are still emerging, threats that can be hard to pinpoint. But Ralph keeps working hard to pinpoint those threats – working to make things better."

Eternal vigilance is the price of freedom, Thomas Jefferson once said. Nader's 80-hour workweeks over a remarkable four decades are all about eternal vigilance.

"Everything I am about has to do with the individual," Nader says. "My efforts focus on convincing citizens that they can still play a significant role in America today. They can take on large organizations and create change. They can improve the quality of their lives and those of others. They can make the future better – for all of us."

Chronology of Ralph Nader's Life

1934   Born February 27 in Winsted, Connecticut.

1955   Graduates from Princeton University.

1958   Receives degree from Harvard Law School.

1959-63   Travels in Europe and South America, practices law and teaches at the University of Hartford.

1965   Publishes *Unsafe at Any Speed,* which makes the bestseller list.

1966   Participates in government hearings about his book and auto safety. The National Traffic and Motor Vehicle Safety Act is passed.

1969   Forms first public-interest organization, the Center for the Study of Responsive Law, in Washington, D.C.

1970   Reaches out-of-court settlement with General Motors over invasion-of-privacy lawsuit he filed against the company for its investigation of his private life. Uses the money to start the Public Interest Research Group (PIRG) and other organizations.

1971   Founds Public Citizen as an umbrella organization that supports a number of public-interest efforts, such as health research.

1974   Wins fight to strengthen the Freedom of Information Act with tougher measures.

1974   Forms the Critical Mass Energy Project to work against the expansion of nuclear power.

1977   Joan Claybrook leaves Public Citizen to head the National Highway Traffic Safety Administration under President Jimmy Carter's Administration.

1978	Nader's lengthy effort to create a federal Consumer Protection Agency is defeated in Congress.
1980	Resigns as president of Public Citizen to broaden his public-interest efforts.
1986	Contracts the disease Bell's Palsy. His brother, Shafeek, dies of cancer.
1992	Runs as an independent candidate in the New Hampshire presidential primary.
1996	Runs for president as the Green Party's candidate and receives nearly 700,000 votes in 21 states.
1996	Publishes *No Contest: Corporate Lawyers and the Perversion of Justice in America* with co-author Wesley J. Smith. Among other matters, the book argues against the idea of tort reform.
2000	Makes another run for the U.S. presidency with the Green Party.

Selective Bibliography

- **Acton, Jay** and **Alan Lemond;** *Ralph Nader: A Man and a Movement* (New York, Warner Paperback Library, Warner Books, 1972)
- **Bollier, David;** *Citizen Action and Other Big Ideas: A History of Ralph Nader and the Modern Consumer Movement* (Washington, D.C., Center for the Study of Responsive Law, 1991)
- **Buckhorn, Robert;** *Nader: The People's Lawyer* (New York, Prentice-Hall, 1972)
- **Celsi, Teresa;** *Ralph Nader: The Consumer Revolution* (Brookfield, Conn., The Millbrook Press, 1991)
- **Curtis, Richard;** *Ralph Nader's Crusade* (Philadelphia, Macrae Smith, 1972)
- **McCarry, Charles;** *Citizen Nader* (New York, The New American Library, Signet, 1972)
- **Nader, Ralph** and **Wesley J. Smith;** *No Contest: Corporate Lawyers and the Perversion of Justice in America* (New York, Random House, 1996)
- **Nader, Ralph;** *Unsafe at Any Speed: The Designed-In Dangers of the American Automobile* (New York, Grossman, 1965)
- **Whiteside, Thomas;** *The Investigation of Ralph Nader: General Motors vs. One Determined Man* (New York, Arbor House, 1972)

Photo Credits

Further Information

- **www.essential.org:** Founded in 1982 by Ralph Nader, Essential Information is involved in numerous projects to encourage citizens to become involved and active in their communities. The website's home page provides dozens of links to other organizations and activities. Essential Information also publishes books, reports and a monthly magazine.

- **www.nader.org:** This website features opinions, editorials, testimony, correspondence, news releases and other material about Nader.

- **www.pirg.org:** This website provides information on the activities of all of the state Public Interest Research Groups, which were formed with the help of Ralph Nader. Information on the national group, U.S. PIRG, also is available.

- **www.votenader.org:** The official website for Nader's 2000 presidential campaign includes lots of information about Nader and his activities.

- ***Ralph Nader's Practicing Democracy 1997: A Guide to Student Action:*** This book offers students an overview of the tools and techniques available to citizens who want to take part in the democratic process. Written by Katherine Isaac and Nader, the book provides lots of advice and information on how to get involved, along with a list of organizations working on various important issues, such as civil rights, human rights, education, the environment, and health and nutrition.

Index

Nader, Laura, 20, 21, 23
  on family discussions, 27
  illness, 46
Nader, Nathra, 20, 22–23, 91
  on citizenship, 26, 30
  on college, 39–40
  court business, 24–25
  restaurant, 30–32
Nader, Ralph
  achievements, 118–19
  attitude, 92
  Bell's Palsy, 96–98
  birth, 23
  boyhood, 29–37
  career choice, 24
  childhood, 24–28
  college, 38–43
  commitment to democracy, 70–71, 110
  empathy, 53
  family, 20–23
  frugality, 76–78
  influence of, 85
  introduction to politics, 36
  law school, 43–46
  Lebanese relatives, 22
  life chronology, 123–24
  military service, 46, 48
  negative views of, 90–93
  personal life, 75, 92, 117–18
  personality, 104
  presidential campaigns, 98–110
  recognition for achievements, 84–85
  relations with people, 32, 40, 42
  sense of humor, 28, 32
  studying, 40
  television appearances, 69, 81–82
  treatment of co-workers, 62, 92
  visit to Lebanon, 19
  as volunteer advisor, 8
  Washington boardinghouse, 9
  at witness at hearings, 8, 11, 14–17
  work after college, 46–51
  work schedule, 118, 121
  work with students, 60–61, 116–17
Nader, Ralph, photos of, ii, 10, 17, 63, 69, 97, 103, 109, 113, 119, 121
  as child, 21, 27, 31
Nader, Rose, 20, 22–23, 26, 30
Nader, Shafeek, 23, 33, 35–36
  illness and death, 96, 98
Nader family, charity by, 31–32
Nader's Raiders, 61–62, 89
National Highway Traffic Safety Administration, 75, 89
National Traffic and Motor Vehicle Safety Act, 57, 58
Native Americans, 43
negligence, 56
Nixon, Richard, 61
nonprofit organizations, 76
Northeastern Community College, 35–36
nuclear power, 80, 81–83, 86–87

O

Occupational Safety and Health Act, 62
oil refinery, 71–72
ombudsman system, 49

P

patriotism, 88. *See also* citizenship; democracy
Peacock, Melanie, 104, 105
Perot, Ross, 101
pesticides, 38–39
PIRGs. *See* Public Interest Research Groups

U

United States of America, freedom
   in, 22, 30. *See also*
   democracy; government
Unsafe at Any Speed (1965), 8, 53–56
   research for, 16, 52–53

V

victory gardens, 27
Vietnam War, 8, 50, 60

W

Waring Company, 26
wealth, concentration of, 102
Welch, Jim, 65

Winsted, Connecticut, 23, 24–29,
   43, 63
wiretaps. *See* bugging;
   see also surveillance
witnesses, harassment of, 11, 13, 14–15
Wolfe, Sidney, 76
writing by Nader, 58–59
   automobile safety, 8, 46, 53–56
   journalism, 39, 46, 47, 49–50

Y

Yosemite National Park, 43

Z

Zahle (Lebanon), 19, 22

About the Author

Kevin Graham has been a journalist for nearly twenty years, covering environmental and other news topics for a variety of newspapers and magazines. He is the author or co-author of ten books. He authored *Contemporary Environmentalists,* and with fellow writer Gary Chandler, co-authored *Environmental Heroes, Environmental Causes,* and the six-book *Making a Better World* series, which includes the titles *Recycling, Guardians of Wildlife, Alternative Energy Sources, Natural Foods and Products, Kids Who Make a Difference,* and *Protecting Our Land, Air, and Water.* Ten years ago, Graham and Chandler also co-founded Earth News, an environmental-based news organization. Graham lives in Colorado, with his wife, Kathy, and sons, Aaron and Lex.

Ordering Information

To order more copies of this book, *Ralph Nader: Battling for Democracy*, please send $9.95 (plus $3 shipping and handling for first copy, and $2 S&H for each additional copy) to Windom Publishing Co., PO Box 102225, Denver, CO 80250. (Colorado residents please add 3 percent sales tax.) Or call (800) 850-7094, or send a fax with credit card and shipping information to (303) 758-3868. Also, copies of this book can be ordered at www.naderbiography.com or via e-mail at windompublishing@yahoo.com. Bulk quantities of this book are available at special discounts for schools, associations, institutions, businesses, organizations or promotions.